I'm on **fire,**
watch me
burn

I'm on fire, watch me burn

secrets to captivating presentations

James Lloyd

9 Screens International
Newbury Park, CA

Published by 9 Screens, International
39 Edgar Ct.
Newbury Park, CA 91320

Publisher's Cataloging-in-Publication Data
Lloyd, James
        I'm on fire—Watch me burn: secrets to captivating presentations / James Lloyd, Clyde Jarrell. –Newbury Park, CA: 9 Screens International, 2003

                p. ; cm.
                ISBN: 0-9728427-0-5

    1. Business presentations. 2. Business communications. I. Jarrell, Clyde.

HF5718.22 .L56 2003   2003090944
658.455—dc21   0305

Printed in the United States of America

07 06 05 04 03 * 5 4 3 2 1

Chief Editor- Tanya Wisotsky Lloyd

Contents

Acknowledgments

"Thanks for the light!"

When first considering who to acknowledge for this book, I was exuberant! Finally, a chance to thank everyone who had impacted my life! What a grand opportunity.

I began by entitling a plethora of pages highlighting periods of my life. I reflected back to my elementary school days, followed by those of high school and college. I graduated from Wake Forest University in 1977 (not Magna Cum Laude, or Summa Cum Laude, but rather "Thank the good 'Laude'"). I pondered my five career paths (thus far). I spent days remembering friends I was embarrassed I had forgotten, as well as acquaintances I wished I could forget. I had listed my fellow collegiate football warriors alongside my fellow Christian ministers. I had included work associates, relatives, and, yes, even in-laws.

My decision was to list each individual who had contributed to the quality of my life. Hundreds of names filled sheets of paper. Following their name would be the specific gift they had bestowed upon me. I became overwhelmed by this project! The dedication quickly became a chapter, yearning to become a book of grateful acknowledgments. This approach certainly met *my* needs, yet I was doubtful it would have met *yours*.

As a result, I instead chose to personally thank everyone I had listed on those pages. I invite you to make a similar list and do the same. If you accept this invitation, your life will be forever altered, and the same may be said of all the friends you thank.

The worth of this gratifying experience is immeasurable, far exceeding the price of this book.

Thanks for the light,

James

Foreword

Life-Giving Fire

Big Sur, California

Of all the places I enjoyed while writing this book, none has been as inspirational as Big Sur. As I sit penning these words to you, I am in this magical and vital place. There is no telephone in my cabin, or a television or a radio, no cell for my cell phone. Here, undisturbed by the exigencies of deadlines and daily schedules, these necessities are exposed as the luxuries they really are, conspicuously absent at first. But now, as I sit in the warmth of the fire, they are things not missed; they are absences unnoticed.

The most vital necessity is the fire. As soon as I arrive here for a long weekend, the first thing I do is start the fire. Before I allow myself to appreciate the indescribable beauty of Big Sur, before I notice the surrounding redwoods or turn to hear the Pacific surf crashing below the nearby cliffs, or before I detect the tang of brine in the sea air — before I do anything else — I build a fire.

Most cabin sites have a fire pit and I use mine from morning 'til night. No matter the season, I get up in the early hours and immediately light a fire. For me, this comes not from the prompting of drowsy habit, but conscious ritual. Those among you who crave the pleasure and solace of the caffeinated bean first thing in the morning (and we are Legion) can appreciate that my urgency for a good fire exceeds even that of brewing my first cup of coffee.

I am drawn to that fire, to its confined and yet unfettered blaze, to its controlled passion. I am pulled to its animated light and reassuring warmth, to the hisses and crackles it speaks as it burns, and to the distinctly sweet aroma of burning wood. And I value the fire even more because I am the architect of that magnetic blaze. Accidental fires happen, but usually sputter and fade. Quality fires require planning and effort, and I build mine methodically and meticulously. I look forward to setting the logs just the right way, to gathering the twigs, bark, and other small pieces of wood used as starters, then to stacking them on the logs in the most strategic configuration. With anticipation, I relish lighting my creation, then sitting back to watch the quick, dramatic catch of the kindling, followed by the lasting burn of the fragrant hardwood. I equally relish the glowing embers at day's end, after the dance of sparks has ended.

Yes, I am drawn to that blaze. Almost all of us are. But why? Beyond the obvious reasons mentioned above, there seems to be more. The attraction seems deep, magnetic, and so primitive as to seem innate. Perhaps it is something in our sociological tapes or in, what Timothy Leary would call, "our inherited imprints." Maybe we are somehow programmed to remember there was a time when fire ensured not only our comfort, but also our very survival. After all, there was a time when most of ancient mankind worshipped the sun, the fire of all fires. It was a very reasonable object of worship because without the sun there would have been no mankind.

The early Greeks recognized four elements that comprised all of existence: fire, earth, air, and water. Heraclitus contended that, of the four, fire embodied the governing principle of life. He associated fire with the soul and human passion.

Our instincts and intuitions still inform us that our relationship with fire continues to be a passionate one. It sustains, inspires, and excites us. Fire is a reality, a symbol, and a metaphor. We dance and sing in the light and warmth, not in the chill and darkness.

And there is a fire, a fervor, an innate spark within each and every one of us that both keeps us going and tells us that we are alive. I was recently struck by our need to protect that spark. While perusing the items displayed in a Nepalese/Tibetan bazaar, one particular artifact caught my eye.

It was an ornately carved and crafted leather piece, designed to carry within it something more precious than silver or gold. It was called a flint pouch. The knowledgeable and well-traveled merchant explained that the monks and Sherpas once carried these pouches on long treks to protect their flints.

Flints create sparks; sparks create fire.

Without this precious flint, they may not have survived their journeys. Fire not only guaranteed cooked food, hot tea, and light, but also the heat needed to endure the bitter cold of Himalayan nights. Moreover, having a flint meant that fires could be given to others to also ensure their survival.

This metaphor was for me both powerful and eloquent. I purchased the pouch and now carry it with me wherever I go. It is my reminder, the symbol for what I endeavor to accomplish in my presentations, and in my life. I suggest you also find a symbol to inspire you, and I invite you to tear out the flint pouch pictured on the page.

I have that flint — that spark that creates fire inside me.

You do, too.

It seems to me that we have an obligation to protect our flint and, also, I believe, a responsibility to share our spark whenever we can. And when we do share that life-giving spark, audiences will be captivated… and grateful. These pages contain the secrets to perform such magic. With this in mind, and in this spirit, I invite you to enjoy this book.

Now…

…Let's catch fire!

Introduction

"I'm on Fire!"

I can think of no better way to begin an introduction than by introducing a speaker who, in his time, set a standard for presentations unapproached by his peers. Several years ago, while living in South London, I discovered the fascinating story of Charles Spurgeon, and, from the heart of his story, both the theme and title for this book.

I feel connected to this reverend for the following reasons:

- Our fathers were both Baptist preachers.
- We both preached in London, England.
- We both lived in the same area of London, Clapham South, and on the exact same street, Nightingale Lane!
- On a personal note, we both have been described as portly and we both have relished a fine cigar.

The dynamic Charles Spurgeon was a minister in the Elephant and Castle district of South London in the latter nineteenth century. While researching this "man of the cloth," I learned some disturbing statistics describing church attendance. During his lifetime, attendance was at an historical low in churches of all faiths throughout England. The average attendance ranged from between five and seven people per service, per church! The notable exception was the Metropolitan Tabernacle, the largest independent congregation in the world, where Spurgeon had a regular attendance of five to seven *thousand* every Sunday morning!

What really compelled me to study this man's skills was not just this astounding attendance. It was the appeal he made to his congregation on Sunday mornings at the end of his sermons. He would ask those in attendance to *not return* that evening so that others would have an opportunity to get in, who that morning had been *turned away!*

I'd never heard of a minister having to make that kind of announcement. What made Charles Spurgeon so popular? What about him appealed so powerfully to others? In my research, I uncovered an interview with Spurgeon that provided, with the brilliance of a few searing words, the answers I sought. When asked why so many people were coming to his church when other churches were nearly empty, Spurgeon's response was:

I am on fire for Christ. And when I preach, people come to watch me burn.

His words are worth repeating…"I am on *fire* for Christ. And when I preach, people come to *watch me burn.*"

Here we need to concentrate only on the fire, not the fuel. I don't want you to be put off by the particulars of our good minister's flame, nor distracted from the general truth of his message. Regardless of the source that fueled his fire, he WAS on fire, and people came to experience his heat, to watch him burn!

I'm sure that there were other ministers in Spurgeon's time that were more learned and better scholars, but they lacked his presentation skills.

Spurgeon commanded an intense and authoritative passion during the presentation of his sermons, and this filled his church. (And though I can't prove it, I feel certain that most of his congregation didn't arrive early to fight for the pews at the *back* of the room.) Likewise, we need that passion in order to burn. If we have intensity in our presentations, it will show, and it will have that same kind of appeal and attraction. And there's something I want you to keep in mind, something that I cannot emphasize enough:

The fire you want burning during your presentations doesn't start by accident.

It has to be carefully, methodically built, and every time it is, people will be not only captivated, but also grateful, firewatchers.

If you're still wondering just how important it is to add that extra element of passion to your own presentations, please allow me to offer you several striking examples —

I conduct presentation skills workshops for a Fortune 400 insurance company. In 1999, I was in a meeting with one of the company executives who asked if I would be willing to help one of the managers (let's call him John) with a presentation he was to do in seven days for senior executives. I said of course I'd be happy to do that, as long as John was willing. This executive went on to explain to me that this would be a very important presentation and that John was an excellent manager who probably deserved to be a director. It turned out that the only thing keeping John from being promoted was his lack of presentation skills. I was then told that if John did an exceptional job on the presentation, he would receive that promotion to director. And I was left with these final words:

"Oh yeah, and you can't tell him about this."

So, the next day, I met with John. He already had his presentation together because it was one he'd given several times. To be honest, he didn't seem that excited about it.

I said to John, "Why don't we really go after it this time and make this presentation better than it's ever been?"

"No offense, James, but I'm not very interested in putting too much time into this. I already pretty much have my thoughts together and I know what I want to say."

By now, I was really biting my tongue. I pressed on.

"I know, John, but for this Monday night, why don't we go for it? Let's put in some good humor, create a very captivating introduction, and initiate a call to action?"

"I don't know. I hadn't thought about doing that much."

"John, we have six more days. We can practice it, we can rework it, we can really spice it up and make sure it's fantastic! What do you think?"

That's when he blurted, "Here's what I think- I think *you* are more excited about my presentation than *I* am!"

We laughed about it a bit. Of course, I couldn't tell him what was riding on it, but he did practice, and he did rehearse, and he did a truly wonderful job on the presentation. As a result, he *was* promoted to director and is probably now on his way to vice-president. I often wonder if there are not hundreds, even thousands, of stories like John's. Perhaps, even for you, it's already happened. What difference would improved presentation skills have made in your past? We may never know. What difference can it make in your future? We *can* know that.

The remarkable story of a friend of mine who got more than he asked for is another example of this. (Once again, the name will be changed to protect the financially enriched.) Robert is a friend of mine who asked me to mentor him, and after a year of diligent learning, he got an interview with a well-respected organization.

They asked him to do a five-minute presentation for his interview. So, he worked on his presentation for hours and hours. He also came to me and practiced this presentation, not just in words, but also in action, actually rehearsing that speech a number of times. We continued to refine it. We worked on the delivery and the timing, pauses and enunciation. We also injected some rarely used captivating secrets that I'll reveal later in this book.

When it was time for his interview, this man was ready. Prior to our rehearsals, we had discussed the salary for this position. Robert had hoped to get a certain figure. I'd spoken to the person with whom he was interviewing, and was informed that the company's maximum offer would be two thousand dollars less than that. I then told Robert to ask for two thousand more than he was hoping to get.

"You might meet in the middle and get what you want." That was our plan.

Well, Robert did an awesome job in the interview! His presentation was so well put together and so beautifully executed that he was offered the job. When they asked him what salary he required, he stated the inflated salary request. The next day, the company responded to Robert with this astounding counter offer:

"We cannot meet your salary requirements of $$$$."

"We insist on paying you $3000 more!"

At this point, I hope it's crystal clear that developing your presentation skills can greatly enhance your career. If there is still doubt, however, please consider the following quote:

> **If all my talents and powers were to be taken from me by some inscrutable Providence, and I had my choice of keeping but one, I would unhesitatingly ask to be allowed to keep the Power of Speaking, for through it, I would quickly recover all the rest.**
>
> **—Daniel Webster**

With a slight blush of embarrassment, I feel compelled to share with you a story of showmanship, which is also one of my cautionary tales — one that will give new meaning to the title of this book. I call this story **"I'm On Fire."** It was one of the most humbling experiences of my life (though your first place vote may go to one of the many others I'll share throughout the book).

It happened in Tampa, Florida, in the mid-90's. I'd recently taken a job with Kaset (one of the most fabulous and fun companies for which I'd ever worked, and where I learned much about presentation skills). I was asked to do a special presentation for the Customer Service Training Department of the parking company for Chicago O'Hare Airport.

The O'Hare representatives told me that one of their biggest customer relations problems involved car batteries. Occasionally, in the winter, people's batteries would go dead, and they would need a jump. This particular parking company had a service to provide that assistance. The problem was that their people would sometimes get the cable wires crossed up and *blow up* the battery, creating an obviously bad situation. The company wanted to know what customer service should then do. They could always replace the battery, but how could the situation be handled right on the spot? This was the help they needed from me.

Well, I decided that I would demonstrate the battery exploding. This way, all the executives could see how well this situation could be handled, and I would be presenting it to them in a way that would be realistic and very entertaining. (I should mention here that I learned magic, in order to better captivate an audience. And, incidentally, pyrotechnics was one of the areas that excited me the most.)

My scheme was to devise my own battery that I would blow up, in limited fashion, certainly, but with some flash and some sizzle so that it would present well and appear authentic. One of the necessary ingredients was flash paper, and I began by putting in one piece, which was probably twice what I needed, along with some added sparkle and other ingredients for effect. I'd rigged up my own fake battery and battery cables, and had an igniter so that when I touched the cables to the battery, it would sparkle and fizz and produce a little bit of flame. I thought this would be both humorous and sufficiently realistic for the class.

I don't know what caused me to do the following, but about an hour before the class I decided to add a little more dazzle and, thus, put an extra sheet of flash paper in the holder. There probably was now four times more bang than what was needed. And

I'll **never** know what caused me to stick in that **third** piece of flash paper ten minutes before the demonstration, unless it was just wanting to really have quite a shocking flash for the group.

I truly had no clue that I no longer had an audience-wowing ersatz battery, but a very dangerous bomb! Shortly into the presentation, I called up my good friend Jim from the audience to play the part of a customer. He stood nearby as I began my performance. As I touched the terminals, simulating blowing up the battery, the little act I'd hoped would elicit a few appreciative "*ooh's*" and "*ahh's*" turned into a pyrotechnic extravaganza, thickly peppered with horrified *gasps* and *shouts* from the assembled!

I will say in my defense, however, that the audience was unquestionably captivated, as everything went up in a flash — the likes of which I'd never witnessed before or since! A *six-foot flame* totally engulfed my head, knocking me backward into my chart, which collapsed with me to the floor! Everyone in the room screamed! I jumped back up and quickly tried to compose myself, ignoring every instinct to check body parts. I immediately returned to the script and mumbled, "Sir, I am very sorry that I caused that problem with your battery. You have every reason to be upset…"

But then Jim interrupted me and said, "James, I think you really need to go to a hospital!"

"No, no, no," I whispered, "let's finish this. We have a break coming up." I tried to pick up where I'd left off, "Sir, I understand you're upset…"

About then, I felt this searing pain on my face. Instinctively, I reached up and touched my hand to it, pulling off a silver dollar sized piece of skin. I announced, "I think we need that break now," and I was on my way for medical help.

My first glance in a mirror revealed my facial skin tone was a burnt sienna, highlighted by humiliating crimson. My hair had caught fire, and I'd burned off my eyebrows and eyelashes. Fortunately, though, everything turned out okay, and I'd avoided any permanent damage.

Afterwards, one of my supervisors gave me an ultimatum: *No more fire in any class!*

But then, Lynn, a coach I had at the time told me, "I know why you did it, James, and I applaud you. Keep your *spark* alive."

I can't tell you how much I appreciated her support.

Clearly, this story confers upon the title of this book an additional piquancy for me. What is now a *shining metaphor* was once a *painful reality.* I **WAS** on fire, and they watched me *burn!* Herein, we find the moral of this "warming" story: Outstanding presentations need passion, but passion needs control.

****

Perhaps passion alone solves the mystery that I call **"The Paradox of Front Rows."** Let me explain.

I now live in southern California, and it didn't take me long to become a staunch Laker fan. During games, I always see the front row seats occupied by the likes of Jack Nicholson and Dyan Cannon, because the cost for those seats is just so out of reach for anyone else. And why not? Your view is at bench-level. You're nearest the action and the players, and you might, should fortune smile, spend a few unforgettable moments sharing your lap with a hustling, leave-it-on-the-floor, professional basketball player.

Front rows are the place to be. Recently, *The Lion King,* one of the top hits in theater, came to Los Angeles. As a birthday surprise, I bought three VIP tickets for my wife and two daughters at $125 a piece! There were several back-row seats available for that performance for one-fifth that amount. I was willing to pay the higher price, because the value is greater the closer you get.

Yet, you visit a typical business presentation anywhere in the United States, and the first rows are probably empty. The back rows seem to be of greater value. Now, would this make sense in theater or sports?

So why is this true of most presentations? If the Lakers weren't playing well or if *The Lion King* was not excellent theater, would as many people pay big bucks for front row seats? Wouldn't most

of them be willing to accept cheaper seating further back?

Are you a front row speaker?

You can be!

Included in this book are all of the keys to making you the kind of presenter who will get people to fight for those front row seats when they know that **you** are speaking.

As I share my secrets to "front row" presentations, there are several things I will not do in this book. I will not patronize or insult you with uncompromising mandates or you-must-do's. I won't detail things I think you already know. I won't talk a lot about charts and graphs or about question and answer strategies because there are already many good books on these subjects. I'm not at all interested in standardizing, homogenizing, or boxing you into one way of thinking. These are your presentations we're talking about here, and there is more than one way to build a blazing fire.

There will be times when we can learn around the light of a small fire that I've built, and then there will be times when I think it more appropriate to just strike a few hot sparks for you, and I'll move on to something else. The latter requires that I ask for more active participation from you. You'll be invited to take advantage of the wealth of resources that I'll recommend to you, so that you can build your own fires and keep them burning.

In addition to having over thirty years of experience as a speaker, I've listened to hundreds of audiotapes and read more books than I can count on the subject of speaking and presenting. I've learned from these published sources, and many of them are referenced in this book. Numerous concepts will be addressed. If I agree with a concept, I'll quote and fully reference the source: speaker, book, tape, etc. Conversely, if I disagree, I'll mention the concepts themselves, but neither quote nor credit the source. No person's work will be criticized by name.

This work is not a book for book's sake. If I believed there was already a book on the shelves focusing on the same issues and cultivating the same skills, I wouldn't have written this one. I'm neither revisiting ground heavily trodden, nor reiterating things already said often and well. Instead, I'm focusing on passion and creativity. I'm focusing on the secrets of captivation. I'm focusing on proven fire starters. I'll show you how to be on fire, so people will watch *you* burn. I want this for you because I've been there. I've been on fire, and (except for the flash paper debacle) it's a great place to be — not only for me, but for the audience as well.

I thought I'd end this beginning by sharing with you a most challenging personal ambition.

My friend Lisa recently gave me the book *The Four Agreements*, by Don Miguel Ruiz. Perhaps she knew I needed these spiritual truths both in my life and in my book. The first agreement challenged me to be impeccable with my word:

Speak with integrity. Say only what you mean. Avoid using the word to speak against yourself or to gossip about others. Use the power of your word in the direction of truth and love.

Wow! What awesome advice! So undeniable in its truth, and so difficult in its living! My goal in the writing of this book has been to adhere to this first agreement.

Now,

If you're ready and willing,

let's attend together

a potentially life-enhancing institution...

...Fire Building School!

Chapter One

Fire Building School

Learn from Everyone

Every man I meet is my superior in some way; in that I learn from him.

—Ralph Waldo Emerson

This quotation changed my life! With these few words, the doors were thrown open. In them, I've gained a richer insight into myself, and garnered a practical wisdom that has advanced both my personal and professional life. I consciously strive to live this quote. It's a statement that guides me in every human contact I'm privileged to make. It's with me in everything from formal speeches and carefully crafted presentations at seminars and conventions, to hallway handshakes at work, and to friendly chitchats with cashiers at the local supermarket.

Clearly, Emerson was speaking not just of men, but of mankind; man in the sense of everyman. Every woman I meet is my superior in some way. I learn from every child, from every senior citizen, and from every teenager (including my own). I believe the best way to nurture learning is to conscientiously stay in the hunt. I try hard to stay adaptable and remain open to new ideas.

By definition, learning is a proactive enterprise. Initiate conversations. Don't hesitate to seek instruction, counsel, or advice, whether or not you choose to use it. Discover people's interests, and get interested in people. Take the time to listen to a really good story, and take note of the elements that make it a good story. And write things down! Keep a notebook, or carry a tape recorder with you. I want to emphasize this. Get those things down that create the smallest spark in you, however momentary or faint it may be, because you never know when you'll hear or see something from someone today that might be of value to you tomorrow, next month, or next year.

Another thing to keep in mind is that you will learn what to avoid. Occasionally, if you haven't already, you'll listen to another speaker and come out afterwards saying to yourself, "Mental note: Never begin your presentation this way, not even if it would end global warming." But, hey, you undoubtedly learned something! Mary, one of the very finest bosses I've ever had, also reinforced the idea of learning from everyone. One time I'd gone to listen to a speaker, and later told Mary that he was just terrible.

She asked me, "What did you learn?"

"Couldn't learn anything."

"James," she counseled, "it sounds like you just learned several things *not* to do."

Point well made!

Wisdom warns us about things that might inhibit, or suppress, either our ability or desire to learn from others. I'll articulate just one that stands out for me. Its influence is both subtle and seductive. This is that particular kind of teacher/student dynamic we call mentoring.

As it is in so many things, there seems to be both an upside and a downside in a mentoring relationship. From my perspective, the hands-down winner of the upside is the person being mentored. When we occupy this position, our sole responsibility and pleasure is to learn. They teach; we learn. We strive to emulate our mentor's prowess and his or her mastery of techniques.

But what happens when you are in the role of mentor? Maybe you have been in such a role and enjoyed it. After all, this is an ego-satisfying position. Being selected as someone's mentor is a recognition, commendation, and an honor. But I've found mentoring to be more than problematic in that it often has significantly hindered my own learning. This may be just my hang-up, but I've found myself so stubbornly in the teaching mode when mentoring someone else, that it subdued, if not completely stagnated, my own learning experience.

An experience with my friend, Daniel, taught me this. Daniel once asked me to mentor him, to which I unhesitatingly agreed. For about a year, we conducted this strictly one-way, teacher-student interaction. Daniel was constantly coming to me, wanting to learn, and I was constantly teaching him.

Finally, I realized that this wasn't working for me at all. Why? Because it was unsatisfying. Especially when I took into account that I'd decided to focus on learning from everyone, not teaching everyone. For too long I'd fallen asleep at the wheel and had fallen out of the learning mode. It dawned on me that genuine mentoring needed to be a give-and-take, two-way street… teaching-learning…giving-taking. Each learner also had things to teach, and there was much that I could have learned from Daniel. I was missing out.

So Daniel and I began calling ourselves *"mutual mentors,"* and I liked that. Now whenever I take on a new mentoring relationship, I make sure we both agree that the process will be one of mutual mentoring. This has been much more instructive and fulfilling.

I've explored this connection for a reason. Like a mentor, the speaker is usually considered the expert, the teacher. With that same honor comes a frighteningly dangerous ego trap.

As speakers, presenters, and facilitators, consider the possibility that there are harvests of invaluable information to be reaped from our audiences. In fact, once we are comfortable enough with Emerson's quote to relish the student's role, massive learning will result. Amazingly, our instructors will not only be fellow speakers. In the following pages, you'll meet representatives from different vocations who have a variety of talents. What they can teach us has the potential to revolutionize our communication skills. These professionals will have their flint pouches with them, so be sure to bring your fuel, and learning spirit.

Learn from Trainers

I learned many of my training skills while working with AchieveGlobal (formerly Kaset, which is, in my estimation, one of the best training companies in the world). There, I was able to gain a thorough knowledge of the basics of adult learning, the firm foundation upon which a trainer can build, both confidently and creatively. And this is significant. I've seen some excellent, creative ideas fizzle. I've also seen what could have been a captivating presentation come up short of success because the speakers either hadn't known, or had ignored, some of these fundamentals that add the essential spark.

Below, I've listed a few of the important truths I discovered as a trainer at AchieveGlobal. These may be matters with which most of you have some familiarity. Some of you may even know them by heart. If so, please consider this a reiteration for emphasis. Some of you may even consider particular points to be just common sense. If so, I do apologize, but I've found that too often what we like to call common sense is not common practice.

　　• There are three learning styles, or modes of learning. (These will be discussed later in Chapter Six.) I learned strategies for connecting with all three of these styles, and I certainly believe, as a speaker, you can do the same.

　　• We retain 25% of what we hear, 45% of what we see, and 65% of what we both see and hear. This certainly has some instructive implications for speakers, doesn't it? This enlightened me about the benefits of doing things in my speeches that allow my audiences not just to hear, but also to see and experience. (Aren't there also some occasions during our presentations when touch, taste, or smell might have its place and be effective as well…Hmmm…) We're definitely not going to win friends and influence people by simply lecturing. (You know, it amazes me that the lecture method is still as popular as it is in educational systems today. I got in a serious number of power naps in some of the lecture classes I had to take in college.) Instead of pure monologue, stoke the fire by adding a few stories, give-aways, group exercises, videos, readings, charts, breaks, snacks, affirmations, magic, humor, poems, slides, props, music, lighting effects, sound effects…and more!

Most, if not all of the time, our audiences are comprised exclusively of adults. And adults learn differently. As a trainer, I gained insights into adult learning preferences and expectations. When you pay attention to them, you'll discover secrets that can fascinate and keep an audience interested and attentive for hours.

Here are some adult learning preferences which are most applicable to speaking:

• Adults enjoy interacting with other participants, not just the instructor. I learned how to set up my presentations to encourage this level of involvement. When you've got the participants interacting with each other, and not just with you, enjoy it with them, because it means they are learning.

• Also, adults particularly relish relating their life experiences and will test their personal interpretations against those of others. Adults want an opportunity to share, and they feel validated and respected when they are allowed to do so.

• Whatever advice you offer your audience is not automatically accepted, but will be interpreted and confirmed, or rejected, through a filter of personal experience.

• Adults expect training to be relevant to their jobs or lives. Usually, you'll have the job relevancy going for you up front. If you can make the training or speech also pertinent to their personal lives, the interest level reaches even higher.

The AchieveGlobal programs I was certified to teach were two-day courses, and we had to find ways to keep the adults captivated, involved, and interested for sixteen straight hours. Everything I've discussed thus far was integral to the success of these seminars. If these strategies can make two-day long programs more compelling, imagine their impact on a thirty-minute speech. They ignite the captivating fire!

Another important lesson I learned from Kaset training is one I call "The Ultimate Rule" — **Be There!** There are no excuses. There are no "legit" reasons for not being there. The group is counting on you. **Period!**

Companies and organizations make considerable efforts to accommodate speakers. They change their busy schedules and make other arrangements so they'll be there for you. It wasn't until I fully appreciated these efforts that I made it a rule to always be there for them. The group is counting on you. **Period! Be There!**

One of the things I do to ensure against tardiness is to never rely on the last flight of the day, in case there are delays or cancellations. In fact, one rumored interview ploy at Kaset involved exactly this. It was a Kaset priority that their trainers were on time for sessions, and they had a clever screening method to ascertain this even before they met a candidate.

In the process of scheduling the interview with me, what they really wanted to know was whether I was someone who would ask to fly in the night before in order to guarantee I'd be there on time.

Instead, what they told me was, "James, we have you on a flight getting into Tampa at eight o'clock in the morning. You're not speaking until ten, so that will give you time to rent a car and you should get here with time to spare before your interview..."

And I thought to myself, "Oh my gosh, I don't want to do that." So I said, "Listen, I'd rather come in the night before. I don't mind if I even have to pay for the hotel room."

"There's no problem," they told me. "We'll pay for the hotel room. We've got it all set up, and here's your confirmation number."

"That was awfully fast," I thought.

I found out later that responsible time management was one of the qualities for which they were testing. They wanted to see if you would come in the night before, because that was the kind of trainer they wanted.

Again, in training, or in speaking,

the number one rule —

Be There!

It might be okay to miss the wedding — unless you're the bride or groom. It might be okay to miss a class or a speech — unless you're the speaker!

Learn from Actors

That we can benefit by studying actors and the acting profession almost goes without saying. There aren't many of us who don't enjoy a well-acted movie or stage play, and actors work overtime to provide us with that enjoyment. Underneath any glitter and glamour, an actor is a hardworking professional. Keep this in mind as they entertain you.

I regularly watch, and enjoy, James Lipton's television show, *Inside the Actor's Studio.* By listening to the elite of this industry, I have gained rich insights into the methods and techniques of this craft. I invite you to join me in learning from these "sages on the stages."

I'm on Fire, Watch Me Burn

Consider the following applications from Art Feinglass's article, *Tips From the Acting World:*

I. Focus. Professional actors don't rush to the theater and immediately dash onstage. No other professional should rush headlong into any situation that demands full concentration. When actors arrive at the theater, they leave enough time to prepare themselves psychologically for the performance. Speakers should also make a point to structure the quiet time they need, if only a few minutes, to collect themselves and focus on objectives. Focusing on your goals for a few minutes beforehand can result in a more effective delivery of your message.

II. Prepare for the role. To deliver an effective performance, know your material well and feel comfortable with it, from your opening lines to the final curtain. Part of being an effective trainer is playing a role. With a little preparation, you can be a star.

III. Speak. Poor grammar, a limited vocabulary, and over-reliance on profanity or jargon can distract from your message. Few tools are as powerful for influencing people as strong, vivid, clear speech. One popular technique actors use to enrich speech and vocabulary is sight-reading. Spend 30 minutes every day reading aloud from some of the great works of literature — the essays of Emerson, the poetry of Emily Dickinson, the novels of Charles Dickens — and you'll soon find you handle the English language with heightened impact.

Deb Gottesman and Buzz Mauro eloquently state additional connections between actors and speakers in their book, *Taking Center Stage: Masterful Public Speaking Using Acting Skills You Never Knew You Had:*

Most people assume that good actors and good public speakers are good because they possess something called talent. It's a word you hear a lot. Performers are talented or gifted, meaning they must have been born with it. Yet, so far, biologists have not isolated a talent gene, and it's pretty certain they never will. Talent is a figment of our collective imagination…maybe it's easier to say, "I've no talent," than to work hard at developing a skill.

This perspective on "talent" suggests to me that we should not allow any pre-existing beliefs about ourselves as speakers, real or imagined, to distract us from maximizing our abilities.

As Shakespeare put it so eloquently…

The fault lies not in our stars, but in ourselves.

Learn from Comedians

They say it's harder to make people laugh than it is to make them cry. So, whenever I get a chance, I visit the local comedy clubs. My purpose is not so much to steal jokes (though I confess to having "borrowed" a few), or even to have some good laughs (though have them I usually do). I'm there to study how a comedian makes an audience laugh or, if he fails, to discover why he fails. I want to observe how he develops rapport and how he establishes mood and intimacy with the audience. I'm even interested in what they do after a joke bombs. I think of Rodney Dangerfield's "It's murder up here, I tell ya'." Special attention is focused on their techniques: hand gestures, facial gestures, volume shifts and, most of all, timing.

Timing is an indispensable quality of all performances, but I believe it's especially essential in the conversational arts. For comedians, timing is the *sine qua non* ("without which not"), and there is no faster way to assimilate this art than by watching others do it well.

When you go to a club, don't let your personal hang-ups keep you from learning from these experts in humor. Can you look past the swearing, the off-color jokes, and even the occasional novice who tries to embarrass you? If you can, you win.

The masters of comedy that I yearn to observe are the experts who allow me to relax, have fun, and to laugh — even at myself. Learn this magical technique and good things will come your way. Think about it…one of the great pleasures from speaking is to see an audience smiling and laughing, and ready for a truth.

Below are some tips from a book I recommend, *How To Be A Working Comic: An Insider's Guide to a Career in Stand-Up Comedy*, by Dave Schwensen. I invite you to underscore or highlight the insights that may be of benefit to both you and your audiences:

> The Amazing Jonathan…has a different outlook when it comes to the business of comedy. "My advice to young comedians is to stay away from straight, generic, suit-and-tie, talking-about-the-difference-between-dogs-and-cats kind of stand-up. That's not what's happening right now. Go to the toy store. Props, props, props!"

Consider this advice from Dave Schwensen:

> You must be an original to be truly successful at this business. In music, we've already had Al Jolson to the Spice Girls and beyond; we've heard it and if we like it, we already own it. We're not in the market for a copy. It's the same in comedy. Give us something new, something unique to you, and we might buy it. Dare to be different. There are no specific guidelines, plans, maps, or rules to follow when it comes to making people laugh. Explore, observe, take a chance, be unpredictable.

> …A very successful comedian with many years in the business once gave me his "formula" for performing stand-up comedy. First, he would record his act on a cassette tape whenever he was trying out any new jokes. Next, he would listen to the tape and write out his presentation of the joke word-for-word, making notes about the audience's response to each line. Whatever lines did not get a positive reaction, or any reaction at all, he would eliminate. He would then take the shortened version of the joke, try it in front of another audience and repeat the process. Eventually, he would have his joke narrowed down to three lines which he could highlight with colored markers on a sheet of paper. Blue was for the setup, yellow was for the middle, and red was for the punch line…

Useful ideas here. Props, for instance (think — Carrot Top and Gallagher). I once used nine props in a 40-minute speech to an audience of prominent physicians. (bathrobe, crossword puzzles, camera, newspaper, printed signs, old shirt, phone, and wallet) And they loved it! So be original. Dare to be different! As John Mason encourages:

You were born an original; don't die a copy.

Lastly, find out how other speakers get laughs. Determine what's being overplayed and what's fresh. Discover your style of humor. Be unpredictable. You'll probably not want to get an audience member to come up and then throw a pie in his face or shake his hand while you're wearing a joy-buzzer. (But you know what I mean.)

Okay, if everyone is ready, let's practice: So…a man walks into a bar…

Learn from Musicians

*I*n Greek mythology, it was the Sirens, who by their sweet singing, lured mariners to their doom. I cannot think of any other single art whose grip upon us is more irresistible and whose enchantments seduce us more thoroughly than does music. Beats and rhythms both communicate an ancient, universal language and elicit fires of primal passions. It leads us into battles, sparks our romances, shares our troubles, and brings us together in times of joy and in times of sorrow. I know next to nothing about the aesthetics or the science that tries to explain the how's and why's of its spell, but I do know music ignites and burns, and that's enough for our purposes here.

Take a moment to notice the uncanny relationship between music and speech structures depicted below:

Speech	Music
Pitch	Range
Pause	Rest
Volume changes	Crescendo and diminuendo
Theme repetition	Reprise
Introduction	Prelude
Notes	Sheet music
Accentuate words	Accent
Rate	Rhythm

I'm on Fire, Watch Me Burn

No other person, in my opinion, knew this relationship more intimately than did Martin Luther King, Jr., whose speaking style must have been influenced significantly by a rich tradition of bringing musical structure into the sermon. His sermons and speeches were also songs that made rich use of every single one of the elements listed here. Can we as speakers learn from other musicians? Can they help us create our "spoken songs"?

Why do we sometimes wait in line for hours (and some of the younger among us, for days) in order to see someone in concert? The music itself is technically superior when carefully recorded in a secluded sound stage. There is something in witnessing the performance, being part of the presentation of that music, which in some profound manner completes and enhances our experience. We are rewarded when we see the musician fully absorbed in the music, when he or she becomes the music.

Read some of the wording in reviews about musicians' performances: "technically accomplished," "passionate," "compelling interpretation," "methodical and soulless," "compassionate rendition," "flashy and insubstantial," etc. It sounds quite personal. It sounds as if critiquing a performance is critiquing the expression of the musician's musical personality.

Actors perform shrouded under the assumption of another identity, while musicians have every appearance of performing under a spell. But what can we learn specifically from musicians, in the context of performance, that rings true to us as speakers? Perhaps compassion, honesty, sincerity, even passion?

When you are a member of the concert audience, you are experiencing the music as the musician experiences it. Musicians, through the presentation of their art, pass along a spark and an intensity that is wildly contagious. And when they're on fire, everyone burns. Watch them. Contemplate ways you can better "become" your presentation and, likewise, develop a finely tuned intimacy with your audience.

Heightening intimacy, gaining trust, demonstrating honesty and passion, like learning how to play the piano, improve with practice.

I learned this from watching my daughter. Natasha has been playing the piano for 12 years. During the early part of her training she was, to put it gently, less than enjoyable to listen to. She produced combinations of cacophonous notes almost as entertaining as hearing a fingernail scratching down a blackboard. (I even nicknamed her "Eris" — the Greek Goddess of Discord!)

But bless her heart, her interest never waned. She kept at it. Day after day, practice, practice, and practice. We estimate that she has now invested over twenty five hundred hours in this endeavor and she has improved with each hour!

She's performed twenty recitals, and I've noticed something a little different with each one. Sure, she's more technically skilled, and sure, she's more and more confident in herself.

But there's more. There's more of Natasha at that piano now. She no longer merely plays the notes…

…She becomes the music…

… She's now a Muse.

Learn from Street Magicians

tep right up, ladies and gentlemen. There is much to be learned from these professionals. The book that I believe best reveals their secrets is *Be A Street Magician*, by David Groves. Most interesting is how Groves deals with introductions and conclusions — how you want to engage your audience and how you want to leave them. Here's some of what he articulates so well:

Act I: Hooking the Audience

This is the point in the show where you do something extraordinary that makes people stop and watch. What you're striving for is not just their attention, but also a higher standard: their interest. Interest is selective. You, the performer, can never command it, only invite it. Attention you may compel briefly with a wham or a bright light; it can be sustained only by interest. Enforced attention without interest is a fine definition of boredom.

Wow! Consider the challenges and obstacles faced by street magicians. At least when we are speaking, our audiences are already there; they're sitting in front of us. These professionals must stop people in their tracks who are busy on their way to somewhere else. It's obvious that we have much to learn from them about creating a captivating introduction to hook their audience. And isn't David right on the money about the difference between getting people's attention and holding their interest? Attention getters supply the big spark. So put some up your sleeve and be prepared to insert them as needed into the body of your presentation. This will keep that fire of compelling interest going.

I also admire the way Groves ends his performances by using humor. I think humor at the conclusion of a presentation or speech effectively combines two truisms —

1. Always leave them laughing.

2. Always leave them wanting more.

Here are examples of some of the quick wrap-ups he employs when soliciting donations:

"These (holding up a coin) are bad. These (holding up a $5 bill) are good!"
"For those of you who are from out of town, the usual donation is $20."
"Change is acceptable. Just wrap it up in a dollar bill and toss it in the hat."
"Kids, if your parents don't put a dollar into my hat, they don't love you."

More rabbits for your hat from David Groves:

...Look into the audience's eyes. The mondo Los Angeles escape artist Mat Cooper makes a conscious effort during his show to look into each and every audience member's eyes, one by one. It's amazing, he says, how it prevents his audience from hemorrhaging. During that moment, the audience members each think that Mat is speaking directly to him...

...Speak directly to your audience. An audience can tell the difference between someone who's just reciting a script and someone who's speaking directly to them...

...Involve your audience personally and emotionally in your show. Use a spectator's ring in a trick. Use their watch. Make the magic happen in their hand. And, whenever possible, say their name and comment on them personally. The main advantage that you have over television is that you're the real thing, so capitalize on it...

...Keep your energy level high. I always did much better on the street after a good exercise session. The harder I exercised, the more energy I would exude and the better my shows would be...

I can't think of any better advice for speakers on the stage than that discussed in these four points. We can learn all of these skills from the street magician. Study them. Learn them. Apply them.

Although this is the first time I've included something about energy level, you can see how crucial it is to a passionate presentation. Think of yourselves as athletes in the days shortly before a contest. Practice and prepare. Exercise, eat well, and get proper rest, so when you get in the game, you're ready and at peak performance level.

Connect with your audience through intimate eye contact, facial expressions, and other non-verbal gestures.

Get your audience involved. Occasionally, ask for someone to come up and play the role of customer, etc. Take a little risk, and see if one of the audience members is willing to come up in front with you to demonstrate the "polished expert" at work. Always reward that participant with a gift, or at least with applause. A lot of learning can go on during that kind of interaction, and it's captivating.

Wait!

What's that behind your ear?

Why, it's an egg!

Learn from Athletes

I want to be like Tiger.

—James Lloyd

"I have always studied great players," Tiger Woods said. "They were great for a reason. I like to find out why they were great. I used to love to watch Watson putt, [Lee] Trevino hit wedges or Nicklaus hit long irons. I would watch how they did it and why. More importantly, I like to study their decision-making on the course. I have tried to pick 50 players and take the best out of them and make one super player."

—Doug Smith, *USA Today*

What Tiger can do will probably be the greatest influence we have ever seen in the game.

—Arnold Palmer, *USA Today*

The other players got no prayer. You cannot beat a man who is stronger than you are, who has more talent than you, and who works harder than you do.

—Lee Trevino

Many people wonder how Tiger Woods got to be the best golfer in the world at such a young age. Perhaps his secret lies partially in a decision he made very early in his career to study and learn from the best in his sport. He chose to learn from both those playing against him and those who played before him. Tiger already understood Ralph Waldo Emerson's words, knowing at a tender age what, frankly, many people never learn:

Every man I meet is my superior in some way; in that I learn from him.

Tiger's strategy was to pick fifty golfers, fifty of the greatest, study them and try to extract the very best parts of each of their games, and incorporate them into his own.

His goal was to create one super player…and for all intents and purposes, he's done just that!

In my speaking career, I have tried to do the same. This process began about thirty years ago. I began seriously listening to other speakers by whom I was captivated. I studied what I thought each did exceptionally well, picked out parts of their "games," and incorporated them into my own speaking skills. I strongly urge each of you to do the same.

Let me give you five examples of my "case studies" and what, in my opinion, each did best:

1) Richard Rogers

Richard Rogers was a preacher who lived in Lubbock, Texas. I first heard him speak in 1977, and he's certainly one of the best speakers I've ever heard. There's no doubt that his "best game" is his story-telling prowess. Absolutely no one, in my opinion, could breathe life into a story like Richard. To this day, my wife, Tanya, mentions that she remembers us on our dates riding around in my old VW van. She recalls me listening to her with one ear, but listening to speeches from Richard Rogers on a portable cassette recorder held up near my other ear. (You can plainly see what a patient and forgiving woman Tanya has been.) After hearing him four or five times on individual cassettes, I called up the church where he was preaching and asked them how many Richard Rogers tapes they had.

I wound up buying all 500 of them! This was a major purchase at that stage in my career. I've never regretted the investment. I've heard every single tape, many of them more than once, and one time joked with Richard that if he ever needed a stand-in, I could step up and recite his sermon, with his stories included.

My ability to tell a story was revolutionized by Richard Rogers. I called Richard one time while I was living in Boston, and asked him if I could possibly fly into Lubbock, Texas, just to spend some time with him to learn a little bit about how to tell a story.

It would have been worthwhile for me to make the trip for one hour of his time. He agreed and invited me to his home.

I flew in on a Friday and shadowed Richard for much of the weekend. I returned to Boston on Sunday evening with some newly hatched skills for one part of my speaking that would forever be changed.

Tiger had learned from Watson the secrets of putting, and Richard had just taught me the secrets of captivating stories!

2) Maya Angelou

Maya Angelou is a Grammy Award-winning poet, writer, and speaker who is also currently a professor at my alma mater, Wake Forest. (I'm throwing in this plug for my Demon Deacons. Fight on!) Very few speakers have Maya Angelou's flair and creativity in speaking. The way that she captures an audience, even in her introductions, is just fabulous. And her mastery of pauses...powerful! Study her techniques and your captivating powers will indeed **"rise"**!

3) Charles Spurgeon

Charles Spurgeon, whom I discussed in the introduction, is my mentor not only in the field of passion, but also of humor. Spurgeon often used levity in his sermons, which was very controversial in his time — and to a lesser extent, remains so in churches today — because the idea of using the pulpit to make people laugh was considered rather sacrilegious. When Charles was once asked why he used humor, his response was, "*I wait until I open a man's mouth wide with laughter, then I pour a dose of truth down it.*" This lesson is the basis of all the humor I use in my speeches.

4) Martin Luther King, Jr.

*Martin Luther King, Jr....*As I write his name down and gaze at it, I ask myself, "Is any explanation necessary?" He is my hands-down *favorite speaker of all time.* His soul, his spirit, his song, his use of parallel phraseology was spectacular! (Unlike any before or since his time) At the end of the nineties, Martin Luther King, Jr. was voted as one of the best two speakers of the twentieth century, second only to...

5) Winston Churchill

An interesting dilemma for me is that Churchill is generally not my cup of tea. And yet, how can I leave him off of my list of fifty to be studied, when he was voted the most powerful orator of the twentieth century? Here's a man whose voice was not only as necessary as troops and armaments were to the British war effort, but also a man who won a Nobel Prize for Literature and his oratory. So much a "man of the hour" was Churchill, that he was the first non-U.S. citizen who was granted honorary citizenship in the United States. In fact, in his honor we have the battleship **USS Churchill.** I also had to include Churchill on the list of fifty because he's my "poster-boy" for speech preparation. When once asked why his speeches were so popular and powerful, his response set a new standard for masterful preparedness:

> **As a rule of thumb, I try to spend one hour of work and preparation for every one minute of a speech that I give.**

Wow! Enough said!

These are but five of the speakers from whom I've learned. Tiger Woods knows the importance of learning all he can from both those before him and those around him to make himself better. What prevents us from doing that? Why aren't all other professional golfers doing what Tiger does?

Why aren't we?

My conclusion is that it comes down to **EGO.** Ego is the chief enemy that keeps us from learning from our peers. Ironically, we protect our egos at the cost of discovering the very things that would make us better speakers. And perhaps that's why the Emerson quotation has been so helpful for me in guarding against this. Once I get in my mind that every man and woman I meet is my superior in some way, then I can focus on what I can learn from him or her. I do not have to spend useful time and energy struggling with and fending off all of the threats my ego is happy to concoct and shovel my way.

Following is a good example of my struggle with this very concept, and my subsequent enlightenment.

I attended a local speaking contest in Los Angeles in 1999. In this contest there were seven speakers, and they were each given three minutes to dazzle the crowd. There were judges who would evaluate each speaker and decide upon a winner. Well, I was sitting near the back of the room, and to be very frank with you, at the time I was quite judgmental and very disappointed in the level of competence of these speakers.

I hadn't been asked to be one of the judges, but I sat there grading them, nonetheless; scoring them on my personal scale of one to ten, ten being best. Most of them were getting scores of six or seven, one got an eight, there was a four and a five. Those were low scores for professional speakers. In retrospect, my ego was hard, hard at work, not asking, "What can I learn from this person?" Instead, it was asking, "What can I pick on? What area can I pick apart and criticize?"

I learned nothing that day.

Thankfully, Mr. Emerson came along shortly thereafter to whisper his wisdom into my ear. One year later I went to that same speaking contest. When the first speaker got up to present his speech, I wasn't in the back of the room, but in the very front row. Instead of my penalizing scorecard in front of me, I had a pad of paper with Emerson's words as the heading at the top of the first page, and underneath it in red ink:

Top Lesson Learned From Speaker One

I sat there, and as they spoke, I learned lesson after lesson. So many, in fact, that I gained more than three insights from each speaker! And I was amazed at what a dazzling group of speakers they had that year!

It wasn't until speaker number five that I realized in genuine shock that this was the *same group* of speakers that had competed the previous year. They didn't have a new group of speakers after all.

The speakers had not changed. **My attitude had!** I didn't come to the event with thoughts of Judgment Day, but rather with the desire to learn. **Ego**. Too often it has prevented me from learning from others.

I want to be like Tiger!

This superstar knows that…

> … **"Every man I meet is my superior in some way; in that I learn from him."**

Learn from Sales Professionals

W *e can learn from everyone! We can learn from everyone!*

I chant this phrase often as this book is being written. I believe this, and the repetition reinforces this truth. One day while browsing through an airport bookstore, I decided to put my theory to the test. If it is true we can learn from everyone, I conjectured, "I can even learn from a car salesman." With that, I purchased *How to Sell Anything to Anybody*, by Joe Girard.

Girard was named in *The Guinness Book of World Records* as the world's greatest salesman. And not just for one year, by the way. He is an absolutely phenomenal car salesman, who could most likely sell heaters in Hades, and the proof is all detailed in his book. At one point, Girard addresses the notion of someone being a born salesman:

> **Let me tell you that's not true. Some salesman, maybe even most salesmen, may be born to it. But I was not a born salesman. I made me a salesman, all by myself.**

Think about it for a minute. This recognized best salesman in the world insists that he is not a born salesman! You tell me, if he isn't, then is anyone in any field of endeavor?

I'd bet not. Do you personally know anyone about whom you can honestly say "She is a person who just came out of the cold and excelled in speaking because she is a born speaker" or "He's just a pure natural"? If so, I'd like to shake his or her hand, because my research convinces me that "born speakers" are the speakers who *work* hardest.

"Looks like Joe won again! He is so lucky!"

What I find most unique in Joe Girard's book is the sublime mathematics of "Girard's Law of 250." He offers us the circumstances of this epiphany:

A short time after I got into this business, I went to a funeral home to pay my last respects to the dead mother of a friend of mine. At Catholic funeral homes, they give out Mass cards with the name and picture of the departed. I've seen them for years, but I never thought about them until that day.

One question came into my head, so I asked the undertaker, "How do you know how many of these to print?"

He said, "It's a matter of experience. You look in the book where people sign their names, and you count, after a while you see that the average number of people who come is 250."

A short time later, a Protestant funeral director bought a car from me. After the close, I asked him the average number of people who came to see a body and attend the funeral.

He said, "About 250."

Then one day, my wife and I were at a wedding, and I met the man who owns the catering place where the reception took place.

I asked him what the average number of guests at a wedding was, and he told me, "About 250 from the bride's side and about 250 from the groom's."

I guess you can figure out what "Girard's Law of 250" is, but I'll tell you anyway: Everyone knows 250 people in his or her life important enough to invite to the wedding and to the funeral — 250!

Now there is a +250 factor and a -250 factor. He reminds salesmen of the adverse:

But when you turn away one [customer], just one, with anger or a smart-ass remark, you are running the risk of getting a bad name among at least 250 other people with money in their pockets who might want to give some of it to you. This is a business-like attitude that you had better develop and keep in your head every working hour of every day, if you don't want to be wiped out by "Girard's Law of 250." Every time you turn off just one prospect, you turn off 250 more.

Imagine how Girard's law applies to our audience members and us. If we're speaking to 1000 people and we can positively touch their hearts, if we can meet their needs, if we can honor them, we did not just honor and touch the lives of 1000 people. According to "Girard's Law of 250," we have impacted the lives of 250,000 people! Picture speaking to this 1000 in an auditorium, and realize you've just affected more people than can fill the entire Rose Bowl twice over!

As we'll assess later, it is impossible to impact an audience member's life without positively "connecting" with them. Girard gives a hint to this formula of success when he avers, "There is nothing more effective in selling anything than getting the customer to believe, really believe, that you like him and care about him."

There's no question that this is essential, but I'd like to shift the emphasis a bit. For us as speakers, it is as important to actually care about the members of our audiences as it is to get them to believe we do. I'm not saying salespeople don't care about their customers — quite the contrary — so please don't get me wrong about that. Again, it's only a matter of apportioning weight strictly for our intentions here, because, as you will discover later in the book, one of the chief fundamental principles of being a successful speaker is to sincerely love your audience.

> "Now, I can't guarantee anything,
> but if you'll wait here in the office for a moment,
> I'll run this deal by my manager…"

Learn from Spiritual Leaders

I'm embarrassed to share with you that this category was the last one that came to mind (even after comedians and sales professionals). I can only hope it's because the selection is such an obvious one for me that the previous sections in this chapter required more immediate and conscious attention. (Yes, I know what you must be thinking: Nice save, James.)

Its positioning is ironic, too, simply because this is perhaps one's best source of learning effective, captivating presentation skills, assuming you choose the right speaker. So, last, but farthest from least, let's learn from Preachers, Priests, and Rabbis.

My involvement (and subsequent hang-ups) in this area stem from my own experience as a Christian minister. Leaving the ministry is far different than leaving accounting, and I'm fully aware that I still feel somewhat uneasy about this choice. When I reflect on my ministry experience, I feel both enormous peace and pain (thus the hang-ups).

After graduating from college in 1977, I became an evangelist with a church in Boston. I later moved to London, England, where I spent the majority of my pastoral career. I am no longer a minister, but as I look back, some of the finest speakers I ever heard were in that church. I learned from many of them.

Oratory savvy is highly praised and rewarded in the evangelical ministry, and when a three-month course to enhance presentation skills was once offered, droves of Americans crossed the Atlantic to participate. And why not? Have you ever seen a large church pastored by a poor speaker? I haven't. The coursework included captivating introductions, powerful closings, and the use of humor, storytelling and effective reading. All speakers were videotaped extensively. After meticulous feedback, there was more presenting, videotaping, and even more detailed feedback. I have yet to witness such comprehensive presentation skills training in any corporation in America.

For this reason, there is so much to learn from many of these spiritual and spirited men and women.

Pardon the cynicism, but think about it this way:

- *Corporate America says, "If you stay with us, we'll pay you weekly."*
- *Organized religion says, "We'll let you stay with us, if you pay us weekly."*

And yet, most companies have a higher turnover rate than churches — Wow! There's so much to be learned here. Most companies are so sterile, so cold, and so lifeless that church membership is worth the tithe or weekly contribution. Also, in most churches, the speaker will greet the audience as they arrive. When was the last time you saw a corporate vice-president warmly welcome each audience member upon arrival at a business meeting? How about staying afterwards to thank them for coming, or for their comments (if these are solicited at all)?

In the critical areas of passionate presentations and sharing personal stories, some of our nation's best can be heard on the radio or watched on the television for free each Saturday and Sunday. Do you take advantage and learn from these spiritual leaders, or do you have hang-ups (like I) that could easily prevent you from learning from others and from becoming your best?

Learn from Books

Reading is equivalent to thinking with someone else's head, instead of one's own.

—Arthur Schopenhauer

I do not lack embarrassments. When I first moved to California, my friends and I usually participated in a daily group lunch, as did many fellow employees and friends. This was a chance to eat, share news, and enjoy each other's company. But every Friday, I noticed they would sneak off without me. I didn't know where they went, and so I finally asked somebody what was going on. I was told it was a book club meeting, and I wondered why I didn't know about it. I asked my friend Marc, "Why wasn't I invited to be a member of the book club?"

He deadpanned, *"Because you don't read."*

Ouch! He was so right! Between the ages of six and forty-two, I couldn't have read more than fifty books (including schoolbooks). Marc's response prompted the re-examination of my reading habits. Thank you, Marc! I was further prodded by the challenging words of Marc's favorite author, Mark Twain:

The man who does not read good books has no advantage over the man who can't read them.

And what an advantage reading gives us. What an awesome opportunity to grow and expand. And what a crying shame if we don't take that opportunity.

My friend Clyde taught high school in the most dangerous part of Los Angeles. He had an interesting way of expressing to his students the value of reading when they challenged its importance. He'd hold up a small ball-bearing and say, **"This is your brain."** Then he'd go over to the globe of the world, point to it, and add, **"This is your brain on reading."**

Since my rude awakening about four years ago, I've become a reader. Between the ages of forty-two and forty-seven, I've read three hundred books. Just think, I've walked around in three hundred other minds! In the last five years, I've read six times as many books as I'd read in the previous thirty-five. I must want to learn at least six times more than I did before! (Forgive me for being a little proud of myself and wanting to share that with you. I shared my "ouch!" so why not my "balm"?) But do the numbers matter?

Jim Rohn sure thinks so:

> **If you read a book a week, in ten years you will be in the top ten percent of your field.**

I've recently attempted something radically different in my reading, just to see where it would lead. I started reading ten different books simultaneously. This synchronicity has led to several new ideas, both personal and entrepreneurial, as well as to a little shifting and realigning in the good old gestalt. You might give this a try and see what happens for you.

Here's the list that got me going:

1. *Taking Center Stage: Masterful Public Speaking Using Acting Skills You Never Knew You Had,* by Deb Gottesman and Buzz Mauro

2. *Adaptation to Life,* by George Vaillant

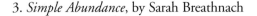

3. *Simple Abundance*, by Sarah Breathnach

4. *Access to Inner Worlds*, by Colin Wilson

5. *The Transparent Self,* by Sidney Jourard (one of my favorite books)

6. *Hidden Power: How to Unleash the Power of Your Subconscious Mind*, by James K. Van Fleet

7. *The Speaking Industry Report*, by Lilly Walters

8. *A Whack on the Side of the Head*, by Roger von Oech

9. *The Dark Side of the Light Chasers*, by Debbie Ford

10. *The Pre-Publishing Handbook*, by Patricia Bell

One of the books on the list especially worth reading is *The Speaking Industry Report-Year 2000 Trends and Beyond*, by Lilly Walters. It is the most expensive (approximately $50) and extensive book on professional speaking I've yet encountered. Lilly compiles analyses, information, and statistics from the three key branches of the speaking industry: speaking bureaus, meeting planners, and speakers themselves. Her first question to the speakers was, "Which book has been the most helpful to you as a professional speaker?" Ironically, the number one answer was *Speak and Grow Rich*, a book she co-authored. It was the runaway winner, garnering more votes than book choices two through seven collectively.

Lilly asked another question concerning most helpful magazines. The two top winners were *Fast Company* and *Sharing Ideas*.

P.S. Ms. Walters currently reads six books a week and has done so for the past forty years (an amazing and verified statistic).

P.P.S. Charles Spurgeon, the minister from whom the title of this book originated, read *Pilgrim's Progress* at age six, and read it over one hundred times throughout his life. Spurgeon also averaged reading six books a week.

Mark Sanborn, an accomplished speaker, underscores the value of reading, when describing what he terms "The Alexandria Principle":

> From 330 B.C. to 100 A.D., the Egyptian city of Alexandria was recognized as the intellectual capital of the world and a flourishing arts and cultural center. The library in Alexandria, itself a wonder of the world, not only held hundreds of thousands of manuscripts, but housed works of many of the world's finest scholars.
>
> Alexandria was able to achieve its stature because it had a strict law. Any ship entering the harbor had to temporarily relinquish all of their books to the library to be copied and subsequently returned. Books were the hard currencies of entry; intellectual enlightenment the treasure most sought.

Alexandria was saying to the world, "Share with me your knowledge." And as we open the pages of a book, isn't this what we are, as well, asking of its author? So read. Perhaps it's true that there's no more effective or enjoyable way to think than with someone else's head. Read. Join a book group, if you've both time and inspiration, because it often augments the learning activity of reading when insights are shared from different frames of reference.

Well, I'd like to say more, but I really must sign off. The library closes in twenty minutes.

Learn from Feedback

Embrace feedback. Seek it and yearn for it. I believe the "ball and chain" that impedes our desire to learn from others is our ego. This is our number one enemy — **our own EGO!** A professional speaker once told me that he only listens to the feedback of a fellow professional speaker. And I replied sadly, "I'm sorry to hear that."

I responded that way because when it comes to getting some worthwhile information after giving a speech or a training session, some of the best and most practical input you can ever receive is right there on the feedback sheets. And a lot of people don't even read them. Why? I think it's that **ego**.

I once attended a three-day training session in San Diego. Overall, it was quite impressive, but at the end of the third day, a participant in the class asked the instructor whether we would have a chance to evaluate the past three days. The instructor answered, "No, I don't believe in evaluations or feedback because I think most times only negative things are said, and I'd rather not hear it."

I was slapped by her response and a little insulted. Did she not even care about our experience? I realized that so many of the things that had upset people probably could have been avoided had that speaker paid attention to feedback from prior training sessions. So why no feedback? That infernal **ego**?

I will say that you should not take to heart every criticism about your training session or speech. There are some people who honestly do not think that they're properly filling out an evaluation sheet unless they throw in some insults, jabs, or caustic responses. It's helpful (and sometimes comforting) to be aware of that.

I suggest you view feedback much like Olympic scoring. With events like figure skating, scorers throw out the high marks and the low marks, and then average the rest. So, when you read…

"You are a God!" — as much as you may enjoy hearing something like that — you have

to throw it out. Thankfully, if the next person scribes,

"You are a Devil!" — you can throw that out, too. With the high and low thrown out, you can pretty much accept the rest of the comments, and hopefully learn from the feedback.

If someone wants great advice, listen to your spouse. Nobody knows you any better, loves you any more, wants to see you succeed more, and who will be more honest.

—Lou Holtz

(with a concurring "Amen!" provided by my dear wife, Tanya)

I recently made a speaking demonstration video. After much editing and modifying, I was given the final cut to review. I had asked several friends at work to critique the video, and they all liked it just the way it was.

That evening I showed it to Tanya, and she said, "I think it's wonderful. I'm proud of you. There are a lot of good things in there, but there's something that bothers me."

"That first clip of you speaking shows you reading your notes," she explained. "I mean, you're looking down at your notes four or five times. James, you don't ordinarily look at notes, and I wonder what kind of impression that might make on a speaking bureau or a meeting planner when they see you looking down at those notes five times in fifteen seconds."

My first thought was, "Why are you always so critical?"

My second thought was, "Let me put my ego aside and have another look at that video."

Guess what? She was right!

Truth is, I hadn't even noticed. I don't know if the people I'd shown it to earlier had noticed it either, but they didn't share it with me if they had. And if they had noticed, I know that sometimes it's difficult to be candid. But Tanya was honest and dead-on in her appraisal.

While I'm scoring points for praising my wife, allow me to share another story featuring her insight. Once, I had the opportunity to give a speech in Texas to a group of CEOs and CFOs. This was an entirely new venue and audience for me, and I told Tanya that I really didn't know what they were looking for, the kinds of needs they might have, or what they might want to hear. She gave me a suggestion that I never would have thought of in thirty years of speaking.

Tanya advised me to get copies of the evaluations, read through them, and then I could see what their reactions were. I was puzzled.

"Wouldn't that be too late? By the time I read through them, I'll have long past finished speaking."

"No, not your speech, the evaluations from last year's speakers at that conference. Then you can see the things they liked and didn't like, and craft your speech accordingly."

Fantastic advice, and it made a real difference in my speech. So, Lou Holtz was right. Ask your spouse (or your significant other).

Naturally, there is a reason that most speakers would never think of asking their spouses for advice or feedback. That three letter word…

… beginning with "**E**"

…and ending with "**O**."

Here is as good a time as any to delineate part of a learning theory of mine I call **The Evolution of Learning**. Learning, as I see it, is done at three levels.

The first stage — "Learning From Masters" — demands the least from us. It requires the least openness and energy, and therefore occupies the lowest rung on the ladder. Most people are willing to learn from the acclaimed experts in their field. Too many of us find this level a very comfortable couch on which to stretch out and stagnate.

At the next level up, we're "Learning From Peers," as well as from the masters. You'll notice that corporate America really discourages this — to their detriment. For instance, if you are a director in a company, chances are great that your company is tacitly set up so that you will learn from a vice-president, but you'll probably not be learning from a fellow director or supervisor. After all, you're above that; you've already moved up the ranks. I'm sure that a captain doesn't mind listening to a general — and I suppose it doesn't matter whether he minds or not — but the captain's not going to seek the counsel of a private. I wonder if corporate structure comes from the military. Hmmm....

I had a great, but painful, learning experience with my friend and peer, Lisa. When I first moved to California, Lisa had asked me to mentor her in training. She was a trainer herself, and we co-facilitated many sixteen-hour, two-day classes, after which the two of us would have feedback sessions. Lisa would ask me how she did; what did she do well; what were some of the mistakes she made; how could she improve her presentation and make it better; did she tell that story well; did her hand gestures add to, or distract from, the content of the training; etc.

These were intensive sessions, and Lisa worked exceptionally hard on improving every aspect of her presentations. During the first twelve months of co-facilitating, there was no doubt in my mind that Lisa was growing by leaps and bounds in her training. It was incredible! And that is understating the truth.

After working with her for two years, we journeyed together to San Francisco to be certified in a four-day management development course. On the third and fourth days, each participant was required to get up in front of the class and do a thirty-minute practice session, or as we called it, a "practice-back." I wasn't too concerned about this; I'd already been training for a number of years. I just really hoped Lisa would do a good job.

Well, I got to do my practice-back first, and I will say that I did an okay job. I don't want to put myself down and say that I flunked or that I did poorly. No, I did fine.

Then Lisa got up after me, and she did a superb job.

She excelled!

She dazzled!

And that was a shock to me. I really didn't fully understand what had just happened. The comments from the group after my practice-back included:
"That was good."
"You did things that we could learn from."
"I'd like to copy the way you did this."
"That was helpful, thank you."

When Lisa finished, however, everybody was in amazement, saying things like:
"You are the best we've ever heard!"
"You are phenomenal!"

And I'll never forget the one trainer who said,
"Lisa, when I grow up as a trainer, I want to be just like you!"

Whew! Part of me was very proud of Lisa, but there was another part of me that felt uneasy. (Could it have been **ego**?)

After the session, as we walked back to the hotel, Lisa asked me, "James, how did you feel about today?"

"I couldn't be more proud of you, Lisa. You were absolutely fabulous."

"So were you," she offered.

And I forced myself to say, "Lisa, I did fine today, but you were the superstar." I was unsettled and the subsequent conversation went this way, beginning with her offer:

"Well, then let's go out and have dinner."

"No."

"James, let's go out and have dinner together. This is a rare opportunity for us to have a dinner."

"I know it is, but I don't feel like it."

"What's wrong?"

"I really want to go back to the room. I want to practice because tomorrow we have another opportunity to do our practice-backs, and I want to do much better than I did today."

"James, you're going to do *just fine*. So, let's go out and enjoy a dinner together."

"No!"

"You men and your *egos*!"

Instead, I went out by myself and had a quick bite, but I spent many hours that evening rehearsing for the final practice-back on Friday. I woke up confident, and I am pleased to tell you that my presentation showed a marked improvement.

Then Lisa got up and also improved!

Everyone was in amazement again. And I'll never forget the woman who was conducting the certification saying out loud for all the group to hear,

"Lisa, if you would ever want to work for our company, we would hire you in a minute. You are a true expert in training."

I remember thinking that day, "What in the world happened over the last two years? I've taught her everything I know about training and she's learned and incorporated all of it. *But what have I learned from her?*"

What I did learn that day was that one of Lisa's greatest strengths is taking fresh material that she's never seen before and, in a minimal amount of time, developing it into an excellent presentation.

I decided that day that *I needed to learn from Lisa* as much as she'd been learning from me. Mutual mentoring – "Learning From Peers." That was the day I asked her to teach me. I invited her to give me her continuing feedback on my presentations. Again, second level up on the evolutionary learning ladder — "Learning From Peers."

Finally, the highest level of evolution — the absolute standpoint on the dais — is "Learning From Everyone." This is not easy to do, and I'm sure you know why. I'll simply refer you back to Ralph Waldo Emerson's sage advice, which I hope you've memorized by now. Like most lessons shared in this book, I also learned this one the hard way.

I was once asked to put together a one-day symposium on the secrets of successful training, and present it to a group of twenty new trainers. This was a workshop I was excited about giving, so I put extra work into planning and preparing the materials for it. I used lots of color on the booklet and, for the first time ever, assembled it in a nice comb binding. The goal was to set a fine example for all these trainers about how important it was to have excellent handouts. In fact, I remember doing a little bragging in my introduction while passing things out, telling trainers that I had produced these materials all by myself and that it was the first time I'd ever a done comb binding, and in response I received a rousing round of applause.

You can be sure that my first point of the day was exactly what this chapter has been all about — learning from everyone. I stated the Emerson quote, and explained that one of the real keys to growing very fast as a speaker or trainer would be the ability to move up this evolutionary ladder as quickly as possible, learning not just from the masters, not just from peers, but from everyone. As I handed out the evaluation forms at the end of the workshop that day, I spoke about the value of feedback as a learning tool.

I was, to say the least, rather non-plussed when I read over the results. I received high marks on every part of the program except one: the materials! Quite a shocker, since I'd taken so much pride in putting those materials together. I mean, I did this with Microsoft Word, for Pete's sake! I even did my own binding. I thought this was unquestionably the best material I'd ever handed out. And yet, when I scanned those evaluations, I saw that there were a few comments about how my materials could have been better. I was tempted to toss those out, and would have, except that these comments did not all come from the same person. Twenty percent of the audience was of a like opinion.

I had to swallow some pride and take my own advice about learning from everyone. I e-mailed all twenty people in that class, thanked them for their participation and their feedback, and then asked them for some specific ideas on ways to improve my materials. I wrote:

Thanks again to all of you for your participation yesterday! I had a wonderful time, and I'm glad to say I learned from you. I am also writing this to ask a favor from each of you. As I scanned my evaluations last night, I noticed that an area of my class that needed improvement was the training materials. Four of you mentioned this, so I could not "throw" out the low mark. I realize this is in an area in which I could strongly benefit from your expertise, so let me know.

Please take a moment to tell me what was good about the materials, and what could be improved. (The embarrassing thing is that I was boasting about how proud I was with that particular handout!) I know all of you are really busy, and I would cherish some input.

Thanks, James

P.S…and I am again reminded, "Every man I meet is my superior in some way; in that I learn from him." R.W.E.

Within twenty minutes, these new trainers forwarded to me ideas that would forever change my approach to training materials:

Hello, James—

I was not one of the people who expressed a desire for "improved" training materials. However, I would be happy to make a few comments:

1. You might consider numbering the pages (as you mentioned) or, even better, putting them in the order you plan to use them. That way, we could simply turn from one page to the next, instead of having to search out the correct page.

2. After receiving your e-mail, I took a second look at your handout, and discovered there were several pages you didn't use or explain. I'm guessing you didn't have time to get to them, or made last-minute changes to the curriculum. We could have still gotten some value out of them, however, if you had mentioned they were there, perhaps quickly explained their meaning or use, and then suggested we look at them on our own later.

and…

Hello, James,

It was nice to receive a note from you. I think that a nice enhancement to your presentation could be a more organized booklet. Possibly, adding a table of contents with numbered dividers. By using this method, you can make reference to different portions of the manual, and your students will be able to locate the correct page faster and in a more effective way.

Thank you again and hopefully this will be useful.
Have a great day.

and…

James,

I think that these were adequate for the presentation given. They were good for us, in that they allowed us to do something. They were perfect to get us thinking, but not frustrated. I personally liked the materials given because it allowed for more discussion than bookwork.

FYI: Here are my years of managing a copy center. The comb for your bindings was on backwards. The teeth of the comb should go to the back of the book. That way there is less of a chance of it coming apart. Hope that helps.

and finally…

James, what I really liked about your material:
- The cover was very bright and caught my eye.
- The name of your booklet was very creative.
- The material was easy to understand.

Now you have asked me for some suggestions, so I am going to be very honest. I hope that is O.K. Here goes.

A few suggestions for improvement:
- Number the pages.
- Make photocopies from originals, not other photos.
- Create your own look. I guess they call this branding.

Nothing to do with the materials, but I think it would be a nice touch to hand out "Certificates of Completion" (with your signature) to class attendees, for them to proudly display at their workstations. Just a thought — hope you don't mind.

Include an intro sheet in the front of your materials binder. This sheet would include high overview of class, objective, what you will learn, etc.

Sorry, James, maybe you want to consider having an expert develop your material or develop a look for you. **

*(**Author's note: OUCH!)*

As you can see, feedback is very valuable to a speaker. As you're handing out your evaluation forms, inform the audience that you sincerely want their candid and considered input.

How regrettable it is: that, simply to protect our egos, so much learning is precluded, so much practice and rehearsal is nullified, so very many changes are not made, and many deeds are left undone… that would have greatly benefited our lives and careers.

Emerson's statement has become my mantra because it releases me from that cloud of **EGO**. Then I can refocus on the one thing most foundational to self-improvement and career development…

…Learning from Everyone!

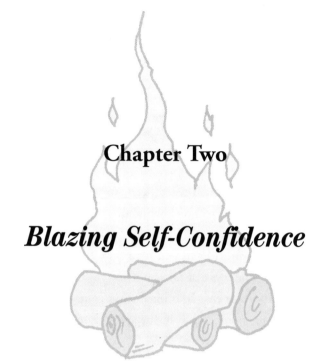

Chapter Two

Blazing Self-Confidence

*M*ost speakers are painfully aware of the important role self-confidence plays in competent speaking. What is rarely understood, though, is the role the subconscious plays in the *development* of that confidence.

The Power of the Subconscious

*I*f this chapter sparks some curiosity or passion within, you may intuitively understand the potential power you possess. Overstatement? I don't think so. Consider a few of the empowering thoughts found in my favorite book on the subconscious, *Hidden Power: How to Unleash the Power of Your Subconscious Mind,* by James K. Van Fleet:

> **…[Your subconscious] is a source of energy stronger than electricity, more powerful than high speed explosives. Your subconscious mind is unlimited, infinite, and inexhaustible. It never rests, for it keeps right on working for you even when you are asleep…**

…Of all the creatures on this earth, man is the only one who does not need to depend upon past experience to control his future. Another way of saying this is that man is the only one of God's creations who is allowed to finish the act of Creation himself…

…Your subconscious mind will react automatically to give you whatever you program into it, either real or imagined…

…It is important to point out to you here that your subconscious mind will not take the trouble to work for you if you do not believe in it. Next, it is also highly important that in transmitting your message to your subconscious mind, you should do so in the spirit that the work has already been done.

Let's apply these concepts to speaking. To maximize your abilities, you must not just *hope* that one day you will be a better speaker, but ***already believe*** that you're a good speaker.

This is the key!

The vast majority of people I train and coach do not think this way. They come in with the belief that they're not very good speakers and are just hoping for some improvement. Of course, this belief is the opposite of what is needed to activate your subconscious mind to produce positive results.

As-if principle: If you want a quality, act as if you already had it.

—William James

For most of my life, I've wanted to be a motivational speaker. Yet, I found that when people would ask me what I did, I'd say something like — "Oh, you know…a little of this and a little of that…oh yeah, I also enjoy speaking…maybe, one day, I'll be a public speaker."

Even in the last five years, after having done some motivational speaking for my company, I'd still tell people that I did training, worked for conferences, and sometimes dabbled in the motivational field.

But this past year, something *phenomenal* happened. I was on an airplane when a gentleman sitting next to me began talking with me.

"What do you do for a living?"

For some reason, I looked directly at him and replied,

"I'm a motivational speaker."

I amazed myself when I responded with those words.

"Motivational speaker?!"

Never before had I answered the question that way. And, even *more* amazingly, my schedule soon started to shift. Fewer meetings, fewer trainings, *more motivational speaking.* There had never been a motivational speaking position in my company before, but that's what I do for them *now.*

It's as if my company was *waiting* for someone to step up to be what I was afraid to call myself!

Evidently, when you say, "I'm a good speaker," subconsciously, your mind makes that a reality. The same is true with the statement, "I am funny."

Talk about supercharging your act and your brain. For one thing, you let yourself know you can. So you feel like, boy, I am talented and I am funny. You can also set your

subconscious to think funny. You'll think of extra jokes all during the day, once you get going.

—Comedian Drew Carey

This principle even applies to creativity. From Roger von Oech's book, *A Whack on the Side of the Head:*

> Several years ago, a major oil company was concerned about the lack of creative productivity among its engineers. To deal with this problem, a team of psychologists was brought in to find out what differentiated the creative people from the less creative ones. They hoped that their findings could be used to stimulate the less creative people. The psychologists asked the engineers many, many questions ranging from where they grew up, to what their educational backgrounds were, to what their favorite colors were. After three months of study, the psychologists found that the chief differentiating factor that separated the two groups was:
>
> > *The creative people thought they were creative, and the less creative people didn't think they were.*

Believe you can, and you can.

Thinking you're a good speaker is the most fundamental step to being a good speaker. I find this incredibly uplifting. Built-in blazing self-confidence. The power resides in our own minds. We control our destinies. *We* can *reprogram* our subconscious minds. What more could we ask for? Just tell yourselves before you speak:

"I'm on fire. Watch me burn!"

The Poison of Criticism

Be honest — when was the last time you criticized someone? When did you last criticize yourself? Did you pass "The 24-Hour Test"? How about "The One-Hour Test"?

Why is there so much criticism? We know that criticism can be proffered with the best of intentions. We'd like to believe that criticism can be very helpful, that there really is "*constructive* criticism."

But I'm convinced more today than at any time in my life that criticism *debilitates!* It works against positive development in *any* area, and *especially* in speaking.

We know now that the number one human fear is public speaking. When we criticize people's ability to speak, it only *heightens* that fear factor and *lowers* confidence.

I've tried to work out the correct balance of criticism versus praise in my workshops. I used to have the class evaluate each speech, insisting on an equal balance of positives and negatives, by having them write down five of each. Rationally, this appeared to be a balanced approach, but it didn't work out that way. It was always seemingly more harmful than helpful. So, I altered the feedback process.

The new format was a balance of *ten* to *one*. I asked each participant to write down ten compliments — ten positives — for the presentation they had just observed. I allowed *only one* critical remark which was labeled — *Opportunity For Improvement*. I showed this newly revised evaluation form to my good friend, Tamara, who has done considerable research in the field of criticism. She told me that it seemed to be too heavily weighted on the *negative* side. I was shocked!

"You're kidding!"

"Tell me, James," she posed. "When you hand out these completed evaluation forms, what is the first thing they look at?"

"They go straight for the negative comments. Wow! You're right! I guess it's time to once more rethink my evaluation process."

Tamara's philosophy of criticism concurs with that of author James K. Van Fleet:

> **I have learned over the years that praise is the best way to program another person's subconscious mind.**

I was once giving a workshop for a Fortune 400 company. I spoke in the morning, and the class was to give presentations in the afternoon. Jane was an executive in the class who told me during the morning break that she would not be giving a presentation. When I asked her why not, she said that one of the conditions of her accepting this job was that she'd not have to give presentations.

"Okay. Fine. I would still like to invite you to return for this afternoon's session, so that you can encourage your peers."

She agreed.

After the last speaker had spoken, I got up to do my normal close-out, and Jane raised her hand.

"I'd like to do my presentation now."

Surprised, and very pleased, I replied, "Great! Go right ahead!"

Now, Jane was a bit rusty since she'd not given a presentation in years, but as she continued, she gained more and more confidence, and the speech went progressively smoother. When she finished, the class gave her a standing ovation! The look of joy on her face was *indescribable!*

As she listened to each peer's positive feedback, she would smile and sit a little straighter in her seat. I could literally see the change in the way she viewed herself *and* her speaking abilities. After the session was adjourned, she pulled me aside.

"James, I was a good speaker in high school. In fact, I was class valedictorian and spoke at our graduation, but it all went wrong when I took a speech class in college. I delivered a speech once, and the instructor *tore me apart* in front of the whole class. And that was the *last* time I've ever done a presentation… until today. James, I saw that you didn't criticize the speakers, and you wouldn't let others criticize them either. I saw how *completely* positive everything was, and I realized that I could safely speak in this environment."

Think of the many years she had neglected doing something she loved. Think of the years she had suffered, reliving her horror at one of our "institutions of higher learning"…

All because of criticism!

Thank you, Tamara…*Burn on*, Jane!

Yet another workshop, another situation.

When I told the class how I preferred the evaluations done, one woman raised her hand and asked, "You mean to tell me that after each speech we're going to write *ten positive comments?*"

"That's right."

"Ten positive and *only one* negative?"

"That's it."

"Well, I don't like that. There are ten people in here and that means *one hundred* positives."

"Right again."

"But then there's only ten negatives."

"You got it."

She went on to challenge me about this ratio, believing we should turn it around and give ten negatives for every positive.

I asked, "How many of you want to do that?"

No hands were raised. Class participants lowered their heads, seemingly embarrassed by their colleague's comments.

She continued, "Well, I'll have you know that I belonged to the club called the 'Toastmistresses'..." (no relation to Toastmasters) "... and it's only females. We started this club with twenty women. At the end of our speeches, we don't share *any* positives. We make *only negative* comments. Constructive criticism! We don't want to know what we did well, but only the areas we need to improve."

"Only *negative* feedback?" I asked, genuinely shocked. I continued, "Do you feel like that was helpful for your speaking?"

"Well, I can't really tell you how helpful it was because I don't know. The whole group *disbanded* within two weeks. We don't meet anymore."

She couldn't even understand why the group disbanded! Who would want to be a part of something like that?

> **Criticism has the power to do good, when there is something that must be destroyed, dissolved, or reduced. But it is capable only of harm when there is something to be built.**
>
> **—Dr. Carl Jung, Psychotherapist**

In our attempts to improve ourselves, whether in speaking or in other areas, perhaps our *greatest enemy is self-criticism.* As the saying goes: "We are our own worst critics."

I've always struggled with this. I've spent too much of my lifetime criticizing and nagging myself! I knew that I couldn't get other people to change by nagging and criticizing them, *so why didn't I apply this to myself as well?* I wouldn't allow people in the class to criticize each other, yet I was *constantly* berating myself:

"If I weren't so undisciplined…"

"If I just had it together a little more…"

"Why haven't I already accomplished…?"

…and on and on and on…

Sound familiar?

It's taken me 45 years to learn this *important lesson:*

Criticizing yourself is counter-productive!

After reading Dale Carnegie's *How to Win Friends and Influence People* for the *third* time, the light *finally* turned on. I had always read this book for tips on how to work well with *others.* The first friend I had to "win" and "influence" was — **myself!** And I couldn't be a good influence when I was criticizing myself.

Proverbs of Inspiration

*I*n a society where criticism and negativity reign, it's vital to keep powerful affirmations available in your flint pouch. These are fire starters.

Following are several great quotations that I hope you'll find inspirational. Cut out the ones that inspire you most. Laminate them. Use them as bookmarks. Post them up in your office. Tape them to the ceiling. Carry them in your notebooks, purses, wallets, and "pouches."

Contemplate!

Focus!   **Burn!**

"We become what we habitually contemplate."
—George William Russell, Irish Poet

"Take charge of your thoughts. You can do what you will with them."
—Plato

"Be careful what you pretend to be because you are what you pretend to be."
—Kurt Vonnegut

"Everything you can imagine is real."
—Pablo Picasso

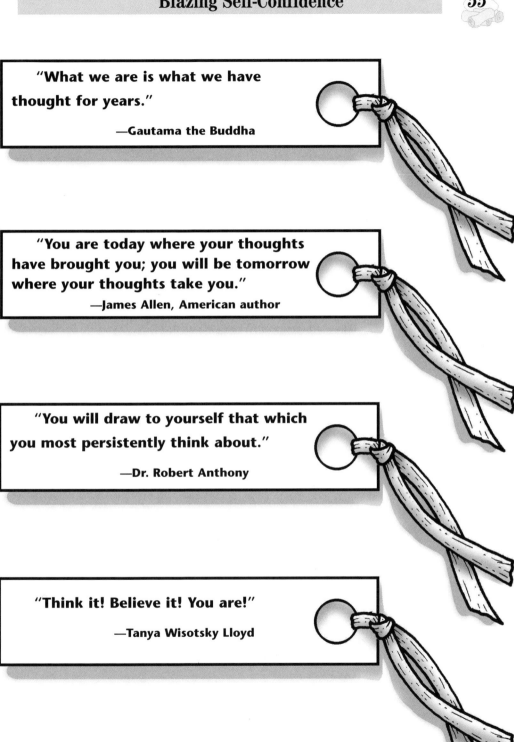

"What we are is what we have thought for years."
—Gautama the Buddha

"You are today where your thoughts have brought you; you will be tomorrow where your thoughts take you."
—James Allen, American author

"You will draw to yourself that which you most persistently think about."
—Dr. Robert Anthony

"Think it! Believe it! You are!"
—Tanya Wisotsky Lloyd

Chapter Three

The Art of Fire Building

There are a number of steps that have to be taken before you can get a good burn going. There's your own sixty-second introduction, the opening remarks to your audience; before that, there's the introduction to this introduction from your introducer; before even that, there's the introductory stuff before the introduction to your introduction; and prior to that, we can't forget the introduction prefatory to the introduction before someone introduces you and your introduction.

That looks about right. Four chronological and sequential levels of introduction that need to be accomplished. Now, we can have a dynamic fire. (By the way, if you really understood the second sentence in the previous paragraph, please call and explain it to me. I'd be much obliged. As soon as I put that period at the end of the sentence, I seemed to have lost it.)

"Simplify," Thoreau tells us. So, I'm going to transform this lion of sentential conundrum into the lamb of analogical clarity. To start a fire, you first gather the wood, then you stack the twigs. Next, someone hands over the matches; then you get it on, light it up. Four steps to fire starting.

Excuse me now, for I must go gather some wood for the fire.

Gathering Wood

There's productive work to be done here. This is the stage at which you take the skeleton of your speech and customize it to fit a particular audience. Very rarely do you go into a clothing store and simply grab a generic suit off the rack and find that it fits perfectly. You need some altering. Similarly, you don't just dig through your files and pull out a speech without tailoring it.

"Gathering" is research, the research that needs to be done *prior* to the event. It may involve making phone calls to meeting planners and to your future audience members. Mark Sanborn, who I've previously introduced, once asked a meeting planner for the names of three people who would be in his audience from whom he could ask questions and gather information. How resourceful! Mark called these people and interviewed them. The meeting planner spoke to him later and said, "You're the *first* speaker I've worked with to ever do that."

You can do more than make calls. You could set up personal appointments. If you were speaking in a corporate setting, perhaps it would be smart to interview one person from management, one front-line associate, and one new-hire. This way, you'd be getting ideas from diverse perspectives. It's crucial that we go to our events having more information than the name of the company and the department. If that's all we have, we haven't done our homework, and we haven't customized our presentation. And trust me, it's obvious to the audience.

When I was a minister in London, we had a number of American preachers come over to speak to our congregation. It was amazing to me that some of these veteran speakers would do nothing in the category of "gathering wood," while some others stood out as quite remarkably well-researched.

One who had done his "gathering" was Mike. Mike was a young and inexperienced speaker. Days before he spoke, he bent my ear with every story he was going to tell. He checked his phraseology with English staff members asking, "Would it be a faux pas to say….?" He wanted to know if there were any English terms or phrases that he could include to gain more credibility. He spent hours and hours of preparation time, and it paid off. Many in the congregation asked me if we could have Mike return.

Contrast Mike with another guest speaker, a man twice Mike's age, who had been speaking for twice as many years and was very popular with American audiences, but who neglected to "gather wood" in Europe. He got up in front of this predominately English congregation and began with: "I'm going to ask you right off the bat..."

"Right off the bat," the audience didn't understand the exact meaning of "right off the bat." They don't play baseball in England. This was a country of fried slice, bangers, and sticky wickets.

He continued, "If I told you that a pair of football cleats sold for 100,000 dollars, would you believe that?"

Mistaking the looks of confusion in the crowd, he blundered on:

"Ah, I can see that really shocks you. But let me explain it to you. What if I told you that those football cleats belonged to Roger Staubach?...You know, the quarterback who plays for the Cowboys."

(Utter bewilderment in the congregation)

Let's count—
1) **They don't play American football in England.**
2) **They don't know what *football cleats* are (they use the term *football boots*).**
3) **They don't know who Roger Staubach is.**
4) **The currency of the country is pounds, not dollars.**
5) **They don't know what a quarterback is.**
6) **And they think cowboys are those guys who ride the range and lasso steer.**

That speech couldn't have fallen flatter if he had planned it that way. But, in essence, he did plan it that way, didn't he? He didn't do his research.

Gathering wood is not a glamorous business, and you probably won't receive praise and applause while doing it. Those accolades will come later, after the speech. It does pay off!

To gather wood prior to the event, I oftentimes ask enrolled audience members questions such as these:

- What changes have you seen in your industry in the past year?
- How has your company changed?
- What are some of the challenges you face in your own department?
- What are your biggest frustrations?
- What are some recent accomplishments?

These are powerful customization discussion points.

For instance, during my speech I might say, "I know it can be frustrating when…" Then I'll mention some of their frustrations that I've previously elicited. This confirms to the audience that I've gathered some wood and that I'm not just throwing a match down and hoping for the best.

> **The simplest way to customize is to phone members of the audience in advance and ask them what they expect from your session and why they expect it. Then use their quotes throughout your presentation.**
>
> **—Allan Pease, author of *Body Language***

I had an experience recently that reinforced for me the importance of gathering wood. I was invited to give a keynote address to close out a two-day event in Visalia, California. Lisa, the meeting planner, offered to drive me on Sunday night. That way, she reasoned, I could attend a reception Sunday evening, the all-day event on Monday, and Tuesday morning's activities prior to my closeout-speech. Lisa suggested that my experiencing the entire event would enhance my speech.

Now, I had my calendar free for those days, but was reluctant to invest that much time.

No good reason really. I just didn't see the need to attend the entire event.

So, I told her I'd just drive up on Tuesday, meet a few people, then give my speech and drive home.

But Lisa pushed it pretty hard, as only a good friend can, and I wound up piling into a van on Sunday with her and her staff.

I had a fantastic time at the reception that night! I interviewed several of the leaders, and got some invaluable material for my speech. Monday, same thing. I "gathered" some truly seasoned wood! I sat there all day writing down comments I heard in conversations, as well as from presenters.

On Tuesday afternoon, I was able to give one of the best speeches I'd given in a long time. Lisa was right! Lisa knew, and now I'd learned. That experience started me thinking about being a different kind of keynote speaker. Without that excellent background material, it would have been just another presentation. Thanks to Lisa, my fire burned a bit brighter.

Stacking the Twigs

*T*wigs simply refuse to stack themselves. Carelessly tossing a handful of kindling into the fire pit yields nothing but wasted time and wasted matches. "Stacking twigs" for a presentation requires meticulous attention as well. It includes such things as arriving early at the site of the event – not ten minutes or half an hour early, but early enough to check, recheck, and connect. Other "twigs" to "stack":

- Has the room been set up properly?
- Are there enough chairs?

- Does the lighting suit our purposes?
- Have we completed a sound check?
- Did we make sure the lavaliere would be effective while roaming the stage?
- What if we roam the room?
- Is the battery in the mike system fresh?
- Where is the thermostat?
- Who do we contact for technical problems?
- Has a glass of water been poured?
- Are we recording this presentation?
- Is our system ready?
- Are the batteries fresh?
- Is that smoke alarm too close for that special pyrotechnic effect?
- What if the "fireball" is tossed in that direction instead?
- Are the chairs in the audience too close together to permit "intimate" roaming?
- Where are the exits, in case of an emergency? ("fireball")
- That group singing and shouting next door could be a problem!
- When does their meeting end?

And on and on — twig by twig, we stack for success.

Assuming all of this is done, the next phase of "stacking" is greeting and meeting people as they come in, being sure to give each person you meet your full attention. Sometimes you'll get some great material for your speech just doing this.

One time I was asked to speak at a private pre-school in Camarillo, California. My speech was prepared beforehand, but I'd never spoken to this group before. There was a dinner before the speech (and may I just mention that they served the finest tri-tip I've ever had). The dinner was served cafeteria style, so we all lined up, about 150 of us.

The audience members were parents of children attending this school. Again, my speech was prepared, but I didn't think I had enough of the personal touch. When the call came to get in line, I took my notepad with me, and started meeting people in line.

I'd introduce myself as the evening's speaker and began asking them questions:

"Can you tell me what you like about this school?"

"Why do you have your child attend this school?"

"Who is your favorite teacher here and why?"

I "stacked" some very humorous and heartwarming quotes. Every time I got to the head of the line, I'd excuse myself, and go to the back of the line, still meeting people, interviewing and taking notes. After an hour of doing this, I was extremely hungry, but I had ten excellent interviews, of which I used the top five in my speech. Mentioning their names, their children's names, quoting their statements, praising the school and its teachers — it made all the difference.

I believe it is important to note that I had my speech fully ready and practiced beforehand. I had gathered my wood. Consequently, I had time to further personalize and customize it with these "twigs" in the final hour before "showtime."

Too many speakers spend that hour putting the final touches on their basic speech and, unfortunately, miss an opportunity to better connect with their listeners.

I've been blessed to attend an international customer service seminar for the past few years and heard lots of great speakers. But I've noticed only one speaker has ever come out prior to his or her speech to meet audience members. That was Stephen Covey.

Following Dr. Covey's speech was a unique presentation given in tandem. Two men from a successful ice cream company came out and spoke together. Sort of.

The first speaker came out and said, "Don't worry, he's here," referring to his partner. "He's just behind the curtain, putting some final touches on his speech."

I thought it was disgraceful to be so ill prepared. Compare that with Stephen Covey, who wound up getting the most rousing post-speech applause that night.

No coincidence…

…Stephen had stacked his twigs!

Handing Over the Matches

There's something dignifying and honoring about being introduced. (See first paragraph of this chapter, second sentence, second clause.) It also presents several advantages. Your introducer can "sing your praises," and this is the best opportunity to have your accomplishments mentioned.

Most professional speakers, including myself, have typewritten large print introductions (our "matches") that they can hand to the introducer to read. I have different ones, depending upon my topic and my audience.

I suggest sending your "Intro" to your "Introducer" to give them time to review it, insert their own comments, and practice it. I usually jokingly warn them against reading what I sent, and beg them not to say, "James has asked that I read this to introduce him."

If that happens, we have essentially just boasted about ourselves. Do that and we've just doused the kindling we are attempting to light. Theoretically, wet wood can burn, but it takes a long, long time to ignite.

Lighting Up

You only have a brief window of opportunity to "light the fire" and capture the attention of the audience. The first thirty seconds will determine whether your audience is going to fully listen and participate with you, or tune you out.

Think of the television industry. They understand that they have half a minute to capture your attention, or you'll start channel surfing. Millions of dollars arc invested to maximize the impact of those opening moments. Pay attention to the "tease" of television shows, and you'll see countless examples of "lighting up."

One question I ask in my training workshops is, "Can you envision every member of your audience holding remote controls in their hands and pointing them at you?" I picture this and I'm determined to remove any of their temptations to change channels or hit the mute button.

Today's audiences expect much more than did audiences in the past. They are ready and willing channel surfers. So we had better ignite a bright fire, and ignite it quickly.

Think of some creative attention-grabbers for your audience, and customize them (through research, interviews, etc.). I've seen quite a few delightfully innovative openings, ones that allowed audiences to dispose of the remotes and pick up the buttered popcorn.

A friend of mine once had the opportunity to speak to a group of 250 professionals who were in an adversarial relationship with her company. In her opening, rather than not mentioning this conflict, she instead chose to go before them wearing a bulletproof vest. She told the group that her name was Jane, and then she gave the name of her company. She continued, " I understand that there's a lot of hard feelings in this room towards my department. For that reason, I've worn a bullet-proof vest today."

Everyone started laughing and clapping, so she took off the vest and said, "Good. I see that I won't be needing this today. Thank you so much."

Excellent introduction. Very creative, and it broke the ice.

I saw another speaker get up in front of a group of salespeople and begin speaking in a foreign language (I think it was French). He went on for a couple of minutes until he saw everyone looking around in puzzlement. Then he paused and said, "Oh, I'm sorry. I was speaking the wrong language there for a moment…One of the reasons that we're not gaining market share is we're speaking the **wrong language** to our customers. Today we'll learn how to speak the **right language**."

Very captivating, as it caught everyone's attention right from the start!

Another gem…

"A CEO was addressing his top exec- utives about budget problems and depleted resources. He'd hung a piñata in the middle of the room and he started out whacking that piñata blind- folded, and hit it until it finally burst open. 'You know,' he began, 'I want to start this meeting by telling you that this is exactly how I've felt for the past few months. Just like this piñata. I feel like I've been battered. People keep asking me for more and more, but the resources are depleted.'

As he picked up the scattered candy and began passing it out to the group, he said,

'Today, let's discuss some alternative ways to meet your needs.'"

Presentations (magazine)

All of these examples capture critical attention immediately. Notice that they employ humor. You've heard the old maxim, "always open with a joke." I would suggest, whenever possible, to use humor because there's nothing like laughter to loosen up people. Moreover, all three of these examples demonstrate a keen awareness of the audience. They are direct and purposeful, humorous and captivating. In short, they showcase the art of fire building.

Chapter Four

Fear Extinguishers

Humankind's Worst Fears

Rate from 1 to 6   (1 being your greatest fear)

_____ Deep Water

_____ Financial Problems

_____ Public Speaking

_____ Death

_____ Insects/Bugs

_____ Heights

*T*o begin my Presentation Skills Workshop, I often have my audiences complete this self-evaluation survey from the *Top Ten Lists*. It invariably serves my purposes well. It's an excellent attention-getter and gets that interactive, participatory energy started. As you can see, I use only the first six of the top ten choices. Please take a few moments to complete this for yourselves, and then turn to the next page to see how they were ranked worldwide for the year 1999.

Remember, your greatest fear would rate #1, your least, #6.

Following is 1999's ranking:

1) **Public Speaking**
2) **Heights**
3) **Insects/Bugs**
4) **Financial Problems**
5) **Deep Water**
6) **Death**

Each year, the ratings are likely to change, sometimes considerably. Death, for example, has been as high as the second greatest fear. Most of the others have shifted around as well, but one response has never changed in the history of this survey:

Public Speaking has always maintained the #1 spot as our greatest fear.

Accordingly, we would rather be penniless, covered head-to-toe with a crawling mass of vicious bugs, and plunging from an airplane to a horrific death in the deepest part of the ocean than standing in front of a group of people and giving a speech. Or as Jerry Seinfeld humors:

So, if you have to be at a funeral, you'd rather be in the casket than delivering the eulogy.

I wondered why the prospect of public speaking engendered such fear and trembling to the extent that we are less fearful of even the "Sickness Unto Death." I've asked many audiences to give me their thoughts on the issue. They answer:

Fear of criticism
Fear of humiliation
Fear of failure
Fear of making a negative lasting impression
Fear of rejection
Fear of ridicule

Fear will smother even the hottest flames. It is impossible to "burn" when we are trembling with nervousness. The three points we're going to examine next are effective ways to overcome these debilitating fears. They are Preparation, Practice, and Passion, which not only make for better speeches, but also are the ultimate Fear Extinguishers.

Preparation

Procrastination is the booking agent of stage fright.

—Robert Orben

Tomorrow isn't only a day away, is it? All too often tomorrow seems to arrive unexpectedly today, and it finds us anxious and unprepared.

Procrastination produces fear, and fear is an entirely wasted energy.

> **Many people use avoidance to deal with performance anxiety. Since preparing for the event evokes fear, they just skip the preparation. Skipping the preparation, of course, only intensifies the fear. It's a vicious nausea-inducing cycle.**
>
> **—*Taking Center Stage*, by Gottesman and Mauro**

If you want to guarantee nervousness, stage fright, or poor performance, then delay, avoid, and put it off! If you want to do your best to guarantee against it—

PREPARE!

I've done presentation skills workshops for one of the nation's top insurance companies, and have discovered that, as a rule, seventy-five percent of the participants come unprepared. Unprepared, even though we take several measures to help prevent this. Every participant is given a course description that they must read before signing up for the workshop. This course overview informs them that they will be required to give a five to seven minute presentation on any topic they choose.

After registration, about two months before the workshop, we send out a confirmation e-mail reiterating our request that they prepare this five to seven minute delivery. Three days before the workshop, we again send a reminder about the workshop and the presentation. So each attendee receives a course description and two reminder e-mails.

And yet, when I stand before them and say, "Now, of course, you all have your presentations this afternoon," I'm met with a room full of confused "it's-the-first-time-I've-ever-heard-about-it" expressions. "What?" I add. "You didn't know?"

Then I hear a few, "I sure don't remember anything about a presentation."

Occasionally, I will get the honest one who admits, "I just put it off. Sorry."

It never fails to amaze me that top professionals, working for a top company, will come to a presentation skills workshop without a presentation! Moreover, these presentations are being video-taped and conducted, not only in front of their peers, but also many times in front of their bosses. Still, remarkably, many do not prepare.

Often, I'll try to break the "avoidance-syndrome" tension by reading those e-mails aloud, evoking some embarrassed chuckling and confessions of "Oh yeah, you're right." (I sincerely believe that if I didn't read these "Exhibit A Evidences" to them, there would still be a few who would stubbornly hold to the claim that they'd never heard about the presentation requirement.)

At this point, the room energy is comprised of a dangerous combination of embarrassment and guilt. So I use humor to make the bitter truth more palatable. I offer the following explanation:

> You probably did peruse the course description and signed up for the course with every intention of doing a good job on your presentation for yourselves, your peers, and your supervisors. You knew that it was important and would be beneficial to your careers, but you still had some time.

> Then you received the first e-mail and thought, "Well, I still have a couple of months to work on it. Plenty of time." Then three days before D-Day, you received that final e-mail. Rather shocking, no doubt, but you didn't panic. "Hey, there are three whole days to work on a five to seven minute presentation. There's still plenty of time to put together something of quality."

> Then it was two days. "Uh-oh, the workshop's tomorrow! Okay, okay, I've still got all day and, if necessary, tonight." But it didn't get done. You woke up this morning and the day of days had at last arrived! Then, clinging to a final bit of hope, "I'll do it on the way to work!"

When I finish, there's the usual "boy-you've-got-me-pegged" kind of nervous laughter. I guess confession really is good for the soul. But why put yourselves through this? Why waste that valuable energy? That energy could be spent preventing that anxiety and those waves of panic. Preparation is the solution. The earlier begun, the better off you're going to be. It's the only way out of the vicious, "nausea-inducing cycle."

Being fully prepared involves more than notes and PowerPoint slides. All of the things that make your presentation possible have to be arranged. Audio systems have to be installed and checked, your materials and props have to be in place, etc. Consider the increasingly popular video-conferencing. It's important to make sure that all of the materials have been sent out to the participants. The arrival of the materials has to be confirmed. Are you prepared to fax copies in case of delivery problems? Is what you're faxing legible? Is the fax machine even working? How about the phone connection? All of this is preparation.

Thorough preparation also includes researching your audience as well as your topic. The top salesperson in the military helicopters department of Boeing's Defense Division has been number one out of the twenty salespeople in that department for the last ten years. One of the secrets of his phenomenal success is that his rule of thumb, just like Winston Churchill's, is to spend *one hour of work and preparation for every one minute of his presentation.*

Once he was given twenty minutes to pitch Boeing helicopters to the Armed Forces in Saudi Arabia. He spent one hour on facts and figures of the particular helicopter in which they were interested — and nineteen hours on becoming an expert on Saudi Arabia, the royal family, and their culture and traditions.

This man does his homework, and it's no surprise to me that he's so successful. The better prepared you are, the better you can handle unforeseen contingencies.

I remember a speech in Pasadena, California. Because this was material I had never delivered before and had to prepare from scratch, I invested about thirty hours of prep time.

On the night of the speech I was confident and excited. Everything was in place; I had my notes just the way I wanted them on the podium.

All was well and good as I prepared to "set myself on fire." But the vice-president of our company, while enthusiastically introducing me, announced, "And this speaker is dynamic…" — extending his arm out toward me — and inadvertently hit the microphone, which fell off its stand, and knocked over a glass of water which spilled all over my notes. He gasped, and quickly grabbed the notes in a futile attempt to salvage them. It was too late. I had used a lot of colored markers in my notes to highlight areas where I emphasized humor, passion, etc., and everything had run together into a rainbow of incomprehensible mess.

Sure, I panicked for a brief moment because this was an important speech, but then my hours of preparation took control. I could barely make out some of my notes if I tried hard; but thankfully, I rarely had to refer to them. The speech went smoothly, and once more I was reminded that preparation is an awesome fear extinguisher.

There are those who will tell you that they don't prepare very long for a presentation because they "don't want to sound too scripted or rigid." Yeah, yeah, sure. I think this is most often just a cop out. For one thing, preparation is an antidote for, not a cause of, rigidity (see next section: Practice). For another, I think statements of this kind are a rationalization for not taking the time to prepare or, more importantly, not *making* the time to prepare.

A speech I gave in San Antonio, Texas comes to mind as a good example of making time to prepare. I could see beforehand that this speech had the potential to be a turning point in my career, as I was speaking on the same program with Keith Harrell, a world-famous motivational speaker — chosen by speaking bureaus as one of the most sought after motivational speakers in the country. I was given a 45 minute slot, and I prepared 65 hours for it. The speech went well. I'm not sharing this story to impress you, but rather to impress upon you the importance of preparation.

My point is not to brag about myself, but to let you know that I started preparing the day I was invited. And, like most of you, I don't work for a company that tells me, "Please feel free to take off whatever time you need to prepare your speech." No such luck! No, I often got up at four in the morning and worked three hours before breakfast. I often worked evenings and weekends. I even worked on Father's Day. Steady as the mortgage. I made the prep time that was necessary…

> …reading
> …note-taking
> …outlining
> …writing
> …editing
> …memorizing
> …developing supplementary materials
> …finding appropriate props
> …and as many essential etceteras as you can shake a stick at!

It wasn't magic, just toil and tears and the desire to do the very best I could. (And I'm still working full-time while I'm writing this book. You just have to make the time for what you really want to achieve.)

Preparation, my friends.

The first steady assault on that fear of speaking, and one that really opens the door into the full benefits of Practice and Passion.

Why don't we prepare for the next section,

starting with a nice, hot bath?

Practice

One day, while Prime Minister Churchill was splashing in his bathtub, his valet overheard him loudly talking. Believing he needed assistance, the valet entered and inquired, "Did you call, Sir?"

"No," Churchill replied. "I was just giving a speech to The House of Commons."

At the small risk of leaving myself open to a charge of splitting hairs rather than implanting new growths, I've decided to separate practice out from underneath the umbrella of preparation. Practicing, or rehearsing, stands alone in effectively extinguishing fear. That said, let's explore the value of vigorous rehearsal.

You'd never have caught Sir Winston standing before Parliament and winging it. In fact, according to James Van Fleet, in his book, *Hidden Power*, Churchill never made a speech of major importance without first rehearsing it in front of a mirror. Imagine the man voted the greatest speaker of the twentieth century, standing up there after the Battle of Britain, holding a page of hastily written notes in his hand, totally unrehearsed, coming up with:

> **Never, in the course of human suffering, have so many owed so much to so few.**

Wouldn't have happened. Maybe instead...

> **Well done, lads. We all owe you a bloody lot, we do.**

Would you want some of the other professionals you deal with to wing it? Would you want your surgeon telling you, "You know, I've never done one of these before, but there has to be a first; so I'm excited about opening you up, and we'll just take it from there. We can share this experience together." How about the contractor building your house or the person piloting the next plane you're scheduled to fly? You wouldn't want them winging it. So, why would the expectations be any different for speakers?

I want to follow up a little on this notion that rehearsing serves to create a stiff and stilted performance. It's honestly quite the opposite.

> **Far from forcing your presentation into a rigid form, a good rehearsal process gives you exciting new ways of looking at your material, your audience, and yourself.**
>
> **—*Taking Center Stage,* by Gottesman and Mauro**

Actually, I once challenged a speaker who'd just done a very medium job on a speech, asking her how much time she'd spent preparing and rehearsing. She told me that she didn't do much of that because she didn't want to sound scripted.

"I want it to be real," she continued. "I have to meet with the group first to see where their energy is, and then I adjust my presentation."

I don't want to be judgmental, but I just don't buy that. If you are incredibly well rehearsed, you're in a better position to concentrate more of your energy on connecting with your audience than if you're wondering what your next statement is going to be. Rehearsal makes you less rigid because it enables you to be more interactive, interpretive, and responsive with your audiences.

To learn to play the flute, you have to play the flute.

—Aristotle

Evidently, the same applies to violins. Take a look at this revealing study from a 1994 issue of the magazine *American Psychologist*—

> **During a 1993 study, teachers at a conservatory were asked to rate which student violinists were likely to become world-class musicians… which were likely to become good professional musicians…and which would be just average. Those who were classified as potential greats had practiced at least 10,000 hours…those in the middle range had practiced 7500 hours, and the mediocre had practiced 5,000 hours.**

The top-ranked students were not rated as "born naturals," but as *hard workers* and *hard rehearsers*. This from the same magazine:

> **For centuries, perfect pitch, the unusual ability to identify a musical note just by hearing it, was regarded strictly as an inherited gift. And indeed, only one in 10,000 people have that ability. As a result of that belief, no one ever bothered to teach perfect pitch. Several recent studies, however, have shown that most children between the ages of three and six could learn perfect pitch.**

Practice! That doesn't mean looking over your notes a few times. Practice it aloud. Practice in front of your friends. Practice in front of the camera. Practice it over and over, and you'll feel that nervousness and fear subside.

> **Give parts of [your speech] at dinner tables and with friends. See how it will be received. Lincoln's *Gettysburg Address* was given several times in several different ways at small groups and social gatherings. He just pulled together the pieces that had really worked.**
>
> **—Brian Tracy**

How are you going to discover what works and doesn't work in a speech if you don't rehearse it in front of someone? I urge speakers to practice anywhere they can, especially when they're first starting. Practice with senior citizens, at prisons (a captive audience), PTA meetings, churches, local organizations, local sporting events — use your imagination. Earlier in my career, I even spoke on street corners, buses, trains, and other unlikely venues.

You can ask meeting planners if they'd like to have a speaker come up and share some words. Tell them that there's no charge, that you have some very appropriate and encouraging things to share, and you'll wind up with a lot more speaking opportunities than you think.

Rehearsing, in my way of thinking, is as much an attitude as it is an activity.

Think how much more productive you are when you really enjoy what you're doing. I myself love to practice a speech. I love the creative process and experimenting with language, mixing different words and phrases. I realize that one of the greatest gifts that I could offer you, even more than convincing you of the necessity for practice, would be to help you fall in love with practice. Romance your rehearsal, and the rest will come together naturally.

Thus far, we've prepared and practiced. We've written the speech. We've rehearsed the speech.

Now, let's say it like we mean it!

Passion

We may affirm that nothing great in the world has been accomplished without passion.

—G.W.F. Hegel, Philosophy of History

I carry a photo of Janis Joplin in my "speaker's notes" folder. It's not because she's my favorite singing artist, nor that she led a life I would recommend as worthy of emulating. She had, in my opinion, a rather sad and tragic life, and certainly a tragic death. But one thing I do admire about her — *she had passion*. Her passion comes through in her songs. And when I listen to her stirring music, I hear someone who has set her soul on fire.

There are many times when I am contemplating making a statement to an audience that may be a bit risky, and I glance down and see Janis, and she literally encourages me, saying:

Say it, Man. *Go for it!* Speak like it's the last time you're going to speak. It may be the hundredth time you've said these things, but it's the first time they've heard it. So, *go for it!*

Janis.

Passion.

That's certainly one of my goals when I'm speaking. I put passion and enthusiasm into my talks, no matter how I feel, how the audience feels, or how many times I've given that same speech.

"Go for it, Man!"

Why is passion the "sine qua non" of excellent presentations? After all, in speaking, isn't it our bottom line purpose to convey facts?

No! No! No! ...A thousand times... No!

Facts can easily be conveyed on a piece of paper!

Facts can be sent via e-mails!

We need more than just facts! We need passion!

Important News Flash! —— If your facts-only presentation can be delivered via PowerPoint by someone else—

You don't have a presentation!

So save your audience some time,
                    and save yourself some embarrassment…

…e-mail your slides, or inter-office your handout!

I sincerely apologize if this "rant" offended you, but I am obviously embittered by the boring "facts-only" presentations I've suffered through!

We speakers want to elicit change and exert influence! Our audiences are active participants, not passive receivers of information. They are asked to make important decisions based on the arguments we construct. We are called upon to be persuasive when we speak.

The power of passion influences people. Period.

Not long ago I was doing research and came across an article giving advice to new college graduates seeking jobs. According to the article, the single most important factor in interviewing is not knowledge, experience, or poise. It is passion. The author argued that employers are more easily persuaded by candidates who show enthusiasm for the job they are seeking. They are more likely to offer a job to such people than to someone with better credentials but less enthusiasm. Passion, it seems, is contagious. When we exhibit it, others — interviewers, co-workers, and family members — are persuaded to invest in us. They give us opportunities they otherwise might not; they believe in our capabilities; they support our endeavors.

—*The Passion Plan*, by Richard Chang

And it's the same with our audiences. When they believe in us, they are much more likely to believe in the message we are giving them. And we had better be interested and passionate in our message, because if we are even slightly bored with our presentation, we can bet our audience will be as well.

It's high time to remove one of the flints from my flint pouch and strike a few passion sparks your way. Contemplate the following five "Passion" quotes. Which one ignites your spirit? Which one motivates you? Put an X in the box before the quote to mark your favorite. The next time you are creating a presentation, write "your" quote at the top of the page for a helpful reminder.

☐ **"Charisma is the transference of enthusiasm. Be excited about your message and your audience will be also."**

—Ralph Archbold

☐ "Coach had that fire that gives great energy! He said one time, he had a fire burning incandescence in his gut. He had a fire about him."

—Jerry Kramer, speaking
about Coach Vince Lombardi

☐ "Success is not the result of spontaneous combustion. You must set yourself on fire."

—Reggie Leach, hockey player

☐ "An actor persuades himself, first, and through himself, his audience."

—Sir Lawrence Olivier

☐ "One person with a belief is equal to a force of ninety-nine who have only interest."

—John Stuart Mill

Belief, excitement, enthusiasm, and passion. How do we discover that passion?

"Passion," contends Richard Chang, **"is not a privilege of the fortunate few, it is a right and a power that we all possess."**

Passion, then, is neither a gift nor a talent. It is a choice, a decision.

I suggest that you discover the "Passion Point" in each of your speeches and presentations. What do you feel most strongly about in your entire presentation? This is the **Passion Point**. Every genuine message must have one. Whether it's a speech on information technology, on finance, or on natural turf…find it! Find what excites you about it. Find that Passion Point. Highlight or underscore it.

Practice it with the passion it generates within you. Make it something you believe in, and you'll be on fire every time and keep your audiences enthralled. The great English poet and artist William Blake was so excited about his job that he pulled these words from his flint pouch one day on his way to work:

Sparks emit from my fingertips, in anticipation of my day's vocation.

(Author's note: This quote has so affected me, it is the title of my second book.)

When you too feel these sparks and this electricity, when they leap from you, then, and only then, should you make your speech.

Passion completes the process of extinguishing the fear of public speaking. Passion will supersede fear and nervousness every time. Prepare hard enough, present often enough, find that passion — and you'll find yourself much preferring to be the one delivering the eulogy, rather than being the unfortunate person whose spark has been extinguished.

Chapter Five

Fire Extinguishers

Fillers

To er is human; not to er, refined.

—Clyde Jarrell

"We…ah…don't …..uh….want…um…to…uh…well…you know…fill space in our…ah…presentations…with…like, uh…meaningless fillers, because…er…ah…they can be…you know…really…like…annoying little …ah…bugaboos." (I would also guess that we don't enjoy reading them any more than we like hearing them.)

"Um's," "er's," and "uh's" are, by far, the fillers most commonly heard from speakers. They are also those that are the most forgivable and, thus, those about which we are usually the least mindful. A few "um's" and "ah's" are not, in themselves, going to render you an absolute fool in front of your audience.

But a demon, however small it may sometimes be, is a demon, nonetheless, and it must be bid its good riddance along with any and all other distracting or irritating speaking habits. "To *er* is human; not to *er*, refined."

A number of people within the company in which I last worked expressed a strong interest in refining their presentation skills. So we invited members of the local Toastmasters club to come in and get us started in our own Toastmasters group. This was very exciting because none of us had ever been a member of Toastmasters, and this excitement was evident in the turnout for that first afternoon meeting. Twenty-five associates attended, as well as three or four members from the sponsoring chapter.

As volunteer president of our new local chapter (a position she accepted probably because no one else did), my good friend, Donna, welcomed everyone to the inaugural meeting.

She began, "I just want to thank you all…**uh**…"

(— "**uh**" — just a tiny filler, a "fillerette," if you will; something none of the rest of us probably even heard)

One of the sponsoring members not only took out a pencil and made a mark on his paper next to Donna's name, but also took out a bell, like the ones you'd find at a hotel front desk to ring for service. He then hit the top of that bell with his hand producing a loud "DING," which surprised us all and momentarily stopped the proceedings.

Donna paused for that moment, probably thinking (as all of us must have) that the bell ringing was a mistake, but then continued her introductory remarks:

"What I was saying was…**ah**…" prompting another penciled scratch next to her name and a second mocking "DING." Things had suddenly become clear. This was no accident, no mistake. He was keeping careful tally of the number of "um's," "er's," and "ah's" which were to be voiced by each of us during that night. The loud, dinging bell was the crier's public announcement of the penciled mark, an additional embarrassing reminder.

After the second interruption, Donna, on the verge of exasperation, said to the gentleman, "Excuse me?"

He apologized, saying, "I should have explained earlier. This is one of the things we do at Toastmasters. Anytime anyone is up in front of the room and says 'uh' or 'er,' the designated Toastmaster will ding the bell and keep a tally. At the end of the night, everyone is told how many of these fillers he or she has used."

I won't reveal to you the evening tallies, but there was a hefty total of effective blows to our egos. More than enough, as I recall. We hadn't been at all ready for the lessons in this "sweet science" that evening. The bell ringing made us punch-drunk; "uh's" and "ah's" pummeled us against the ropes, working the body and buckling the legs. No "ding" was spared; no speaker spoiled; and we all left the ring humbled and more than a little mortified.

I enjoy Toastmasters and can recommend them to you without hesitation. It's truly a great organization, a place where one can receive education and practice in speaking for very little financial investment. But this dinging considerably bothered me.

That week I called up the governor of Toastmasters for my county. After introducing myself, I explained, "I'm a brand new member and have just attended my first and only meeting a few days ago. I really love the organization and I feel it offers great promise to those coming to our new chapter, but I have one serious concern…"

Before I could say more, he said, "Let me guess. Is it that bell?"

I quickly confirmed his guess. He told me that most new members have great trouble with the bell. In answer to whether it was necessary, he maintained that by the time we're adults, "um's" and "ah's" are so inherent, so commonplace, so ingrained in our speaking process, that it takes radical surgery to get them out.

"That bell," he concluded, "is the radical surgery."

Looking back, I now agree.

The proper cure is rarely the most pleasant, and although I've never grown to fully appreciate that bell dinging during speeches, I cannot deny its value as a surgical device. I remember how embarrassed Donna was when, at the end of that first meeting, the man announced, "Donna, thirty-four."

But the next week it was, "Donna, twenty-seven."

Then, "Sixteen."

I'll never forget the night the man shouted out, "Donna, eight," and she victoriously exclaimed to the group, "Single digits!"

That bell was indeed working. And the more we kept its noisy little mouth shut, the more successful the surgical procedure was.

It's important to recognize that fillers can be as distracting to your audiences as the Toastmasters dinging bell would be to you during your speeches. I once worked for a company that had an executive notorious for his excessive use of meaningless audibles during conference calls. In fact, one off-site office would literally tally his "ah's" and "er's" on the chalkboard while he spoke – sometimes going so far as to wager how many this executive would make during that call.

I can assure you of one thing. If people are spending their time doing that sort of thing, they surely aren't paying attention to the content of your discussion or speech. The level of distraction caused by fillers is, at this point, extreme, and whatever cogent and innovative ideas you had might have been more effectively publicized in an inter-office memo.

Why do we speakers prefer something to nothing? Why choose distracting meaningless fillers ("ah," "um," "er") over potentially meaningful silence ("..............")?

I tend to believe it's because we are intimidated by empty spaces when we speak. We fear pauses because they seem awkward and counterproductive; we associate silence with dead air. What we don't understand is that we can use "emptiness" to our advantage. It's those distracting audible pauses which really do constitute dead air, but appropriate silences can be employed both engagingly and productively.

One of the greatest tools of dynamic speaking is the nicely placed inaudible pause because it can create that bit of tension when everyone is riveted. Your audience often needs silent moments during your speech so they can absorb important points you've made. When your words resonate, an effective pause allows the audience to appreciate the echoes.

I encourage you to join Toastmasters because they are dedicated to eliminating those naughty fillers and making you a better speaker. And, when you join, take a little advice from one who knows. When you're up there in front of everyone and giving your speech:

Ask not for whom the bell dings...

...it dings for thee!

Arrogance

G*eneral James Garfield* (later to become the twentieth U.S. President) once visited the Metropolitan Tabernacle to listen to Reverend Spurgeon. He wanted to "discover what manner of man he was, and what was the secret of his power." His observations were printed in the 1883 volume of *Century Magazine:*

> **His manner is exceedingly simple and unaffected. He does not appear to be aware that he is doing a great thing, and I could see no indication that his success has turned his head.**

According to the *Speaker's Industry Report*, today's presenters have much to learn from Spurgeon. The question offered to meeting planners was—

"What things would you like to tell speakers but are too polite or intimidated to say or ask?" The first three answers from these professionals were:

1. "You are cocky and smug."

2. "You are not God!"

3. "Believe it or not, you work for me. I am a customer."

Please speakers, don't brag about your accomplishments! If your achievements need to be extolled, let someone else — the introducer, for instance — do the bragging for you. It's much more to your credit and is much better received by your audience.

I once heard a National Basketball Association Hall-of-Famer give a presentation to one thousand people. At the beginning of his presentation, he started listing all of his incredible accomplishments, and I soon began to sense a marked lowering of excitement and energy level among the assembled.

Why? He wasn't exaggerating; everything he said was undeniably true, yet he was immediately perceived as arrogant. As speakers, it matters less who we are, and much more who we are perceived to be. This former basketball great may in fact be a very modest and self-effacing man when he's not at "center court," but on that day he came across to his audience as a braggart, plain and simple. And nobody wants to listen to a braggart. He had already lost a vital connection with his audience. He'd set them up to concentrate on looking for mistakes in his presentation. They were no longer as interested in his message as they were in giving him their own — "You're not so great." When you allow your introducer to tell the audience how great you are, it's complimentary; when you do it yourself, it's arrogance.

Now, if you must mention your accomplishments (and perhaps occasionally it's justified), at least add a dollop of humor and/or a touch of class. Provide a sensible explanation to your audience for its presence. I did witness a professional speaker who accomplished this with style and understandable purpose. She stopped in the middle of her speech, after she had done some bragging about herself, and told her audience, "I'm not telling you this story to *impress you*, but rather to *impress upon you* the importance of…"

Nice technique, much more effective, and a good way of maintaining rapport. Again, though, it is a good idea to have somebody else do that boasting about you.

I do not believe that most speakers simply set out to impress audiences with a list of their own honors and achievements. The most likely explanation is that it's a misguided attempt to establish immediate credibility.

This method fails for three reasons…

• First, it's almost invariably seen as arrogance, which destroys credibility rather than builds it.

• Second, credibility is rebuilt with each presentation. In this sense, you're only as good as what you do today. What you did five years ago looks good in your trophy case, but tonight is what counts tonight.

• Third, bragging focuses the spotlight only on the speaker, while the audience sits in the dark. What you want to do is empower your audience, and shine the light on them:

> **The greatest good we can do for others is not to share our riches, but to reveal their.**
>
> **—Benjamin Disraeli**

When you boast about yourself, you're not on fire. You simply go up in smoke. I love Mark Sanborn's two-point personal mantra that helps safeguard against arrogance at the podium:

Help me to serve – not just to shine.

Help me empower – not just impress.

Mark's mantra is succinct and profound, and worth committing to memory. I wrote an article for a training publication revealing my personal anti-arrogance protection strategy, and will conclude this section by sharing it with you.

"Ah, there you are."

There are two types of people — those who come into a room and say, "Well, here I am," and those who come in and say, "Ah, there you are."

—Frederick Collins

I have this quote taped inside my leather note folder. Whether I'm speaking or training, my eyes occasionally glance at its wisdom, and I am again reminded. I'm reminded that my class, my audience, my listeners…*they* are *my* customers! While I am challenging my class to dazzle their customers, I have a golden opportunity to model this magical principle for mine.

Sometimes it is very difficult to do this: dozing participants, late-comers, those who disagree with me, those who disagree with each other, those who disagree with the material, side conversations, complainers, those who return late from breaks, and those who do not even return from breaks.

I hear…

"You know who really needs this training?"

"Can I keep this toy?"

"This room is too hot!"

Usually followed by…

"Now it's too cold!

I am reminded that every day my participants face similar challenges with their customers. Perhaps if I can demonstrate the power of gratitude, composure, and respect, they will do the same.

So, the next time you enter a room,

> *smile,*

> > and say,

"Ah, there you are!"

Overtime

Stand up so you'll be seen. Speak up so you'll be heard. And then sit down so you'll be appreciated.

—John Davies, Speaker and Trainer

Ready for a stiff challenge? I submit there is a direct correlation between the overtime minutes of a speech and the speaker's ego! If you just had a distinctly negative reaction to this theory, the red warning ego light may be *flashing—*

Ego! Ego!

Addressing an audience is a blessing; not stopping in time is a curse. "Leave 'em wanting more" is an adage most speakers can quote, but few can follow. Even when we know that it is always advantageous to cease while the fire is still hot, the dreaded ego too often has the last word (or words).

While I was visiting a friend in Texas, a speaker I know invited me to sit in on his Saturday morning class. This presentation skills workshop was scheduled from eleven to noon. The class was fantastic, and we were all involved and learning a great deal.

However, high noon was approaching quickly, and I noticed that people were getting just a little bit antsy. The bell to end class rang at noon, and the teacher went on as if he hadn't even heard it. Students still listened to him, but I could sense a significant energy change. A few of them began gathering their books together and looking at their watches as polite signals to the teacher that it was time to go.

He continued to speak. Ten minutes later the late-bell sounded. He responded that he had one more thing to say regarding this…and another regarding that… He talked on until about twelve-twenty, when all of a sudden he paused and said, "How's everybody feeling right now?"

There wasn't a word in response.

"Please be honest," he said. "How is everybody feeling right now about the fact that this class went twenty minutes late?"

Finally, it began to come out.

"Well, I'll be honest with you. I really like your class and always look forward to it, but this is kind of an inconvenience for me. I had a twelve o'clock appointment with someone."

Someone else added, "My wife has been upstairs for twenty minutes! She always picks me up at twelve, and we go out and have lunch together."

Similar comments were also made. The teacher then surprised us all by informing us that he had held us overtime *on purpose*, adding that he would never again hold us past twelve o'clock.

"But as future preachers and teachers," he concluded, "I want you to remember how this feels. I want you to remember how important it is *not to keep people overtime*."

This was a major lesson for me because, even though he was one of the most enthralling speakers I knew, people resented even him for going overtime.

I know other truly exceptional, captivating speakers who have yet to get their brains wrapped around this essential. One excellent speaker, a man who had been one of my mentors, immediately comes to mind. He is the charismatic, standing-ovation kind of performer who really knows how to work his magic on an audience.

But he oftentimes went long. When I've been in the audience when this happened, I've seen positive energy deteriorate. Applause became forced. Ovations were few and lethargic, given more from a sense of obligation than inspiration.

Given the chance, the audience will let you know in no uncertain terms that they don't appreciate you holding them overtime.

I was once in a seminar group of twenty, listening to a woman who told us early on that lunch would be at twelve o'clock. She was a captivating speaker. Noon came and we were ready to stop. Noon went, and with it, a lot of enthusiasm.

"Oh, I have just a couple more stories to share with you before lunch," she said. Twelve-thirty. Uneasiness grew.

"Now, I'd like to read a poem before we break." (A long poem followed by another couple of stories.) I could have sworn I heard the gnashing of teeth.

"Oh yeah, that reminds me of another story."

We finally broke for lunch at one-twenty in the afternoon! I sat eating with three other audience members and heard someone comment,

"You know, I think she really loves to hear her own voice."

F.Y.I. My wife, who is also *chief* editor, begged and pleaded for me to delete that last quote out of this book. After I refused to erase it, she asked that I at least remove the **bold typeface.** When I again defiantly held my ground, she challenged me, "Why are you so desperately clinging to that thought?"

"Tanya, this is a crucial truth! This is as important as *any* lesson in this book:

When speakers fall in love with their *own* stories, their *own* wisdom, and even their *own* voices…
>   …*that signals the birth of* **EGO**,
>   …*that signals the death of humility.*

When this happens, you can *forget* connecting with an audience!

When this happens, you can *forget* captivating an audience!

These arrogant speakers are thinking —
*'I'm on fire, and when I speak, I enjoy watching **myself** burn.'"*

Tanya quickly urged, "That's good! Write *that* down!"

And so I did!

Back to the story—

"You know, I think she really loves to hear her own voice."

When I heard that, instead of just being critical of this particular speaker, I applied it to myself. I wondered how often I simply wanted to hear my own voice, tell the last tale, make that extra analogy at the audience's expense and, ultimately, at my expense. I noticed how this audience expressed their displeasure. We'd been given an hour lunch. Very few came back on time. Most came back late enough to make a point:

You didn't honor our time. Why should we honor yours?

Ready for a second challenge? This one will separate you from the majority of fellow speakers. Make it a point to end your speech a few minutes *before* the scheduled time. It's a way of acknowledging the importance of your audience's time, also showcasing your discipline and humility.

As a timing tip, if you wear a watch, consider wearing it with the face on the inside of your wrist. Try it the normal way and discreetly try to check the time. Hard isn't it? Now try it on the inside, you give a discreet glance at your wrist, and nobody knows.

—*Secrets of Successful Speakers*, by Lilly Walters

I oftentimes like to ask a friend, an organizer, or even someone in the audience I just interviewed, to time my presentations. I'll ask for both a ten-minute warning and a three-minute warning. I've never had anyone turn me down, and they usually enjoy and take pride in their part of the presentation.

If there's to be watch-watching in the audience, you want it to be the result of the positive connection you've created with them. You want them saying, "Is that all? I could have heard her for another hour! It can't be time to go yet." To me, that's the ideal in terms of timing.

You simply cannot allow yourself to have an audience captivated for fifty minutes, only to leave them grumbling and disappointed for the silly reason that you went overtime. Close the magic shop early. Leave them wanting more. Leave them wanting to hear your next story even more than you want to tell it.

Lecturing

Lecture not, for the vestments of sagacity ill behoove you.

From the Book of *Lloyd* 12:7   (King *James* Version)

Unless you're a preacher, don't sermonize. Unless you're a Caesar, don't pontificate. We cannot "burn" by means of proclamation, only through captivation. My experience has taught me that lecturing is a potent extinguisher. When we, instead, ask questions, interact with the audience, and allow the audience to interact with one another, captivating sparks are created. When those sparks flare and fly throughout the presentation, you can more correctly say, "*I came. I saw. I burned.*"

"Telling is the most futile thing there is. It compresses, represses, and depresses," maintains Joe Badin. **"Asking empowers, enhances, and expands."**

I once gave a speech for 500 childcare professionals who worked with low-income parents. For spark, I used a book about children entitled *If I Were President*, by Bill Adler. In it, children humorously address the office and power of the President. I read an example to the audience:

> Bobby, aged seven, and from Jamaica Plains, MA, claimed, "If I were President, I would send every girl in my class to the moon...except Jennifer."

I then said, "I'm wondering what *you* would do if you were the President. Let me get some thoughts from the crowd."

As I wandered through the audience, people raised their hands to speak. I had them voice their opinions into my microphone. Talk about crowd involvement and participation! They made comments on all aspects of their work, about people being underpaid, about those being under-appreciated, about laws that should be stricter, etc. There was resounding applause after each comment! They were applauding *each other's* suggestions!

I had never experienced a more dynamic speaker-audience connection. And it happened because I was asking questions, and honoring other's views instead of focusing exclusively on conveying my own. "Lecture not..."

In September of 1999, there was an article in my local Southern California paper, *The Star*, regarding an ethnic training program given to law enforcement officers. The program had been met with formidable resistance.

Here were some comments from the officers:
"We in the force do a great job without this course."
"I guarantee that many in the force don't believe that this program works."

Here were some comments from the trainer:
"You can feel the tension."
"They roll their eyes."

"They sigh heavily, projecting boredom."

"They do not want to be there."

Now, there may be a number of reasons for the officers' oppositions to that program, but there were other statements in the article I think worthy of note:

"This course is mandated by the state of California."

"We should just keep hammering it on them…"

"She lectures officers on the need to respect…"

Mandated?

Hammering?

Lectures?

(Hmmm…Do we really wonder why this course hadn't been better received?)

In the first chapter, I discussed the distinction between lecturing and facilitating. We don't always want to be the "Sage on the Stage." Sometimes being the "Guide on the Side" is more effective. Adult learning styles insist that what you're presenting be relevant to them and to their betterment. Clearly, our audiences want and deserve our respect. One way we can accomplish this is by truly involving them in the learning process.

If you tell me, I may listen.

If you show me, I may understand.

If you involve me, I will learn.

—Confucius

Hypocrisy

We, who were to lay the foundations of kindness, could not ourselves be kind.

—From a poem by Bertold Brecht

Clyde, a friend of mine, was an educational counselor working with disenfranchised, "at risk" students in high school dropout recovery programs. He had the above quotation mounted on the wall of his office as a behavioral and spiritual reminder.

As speakers and trainers, we have to be more attuned to how we represent ourselves than do those in professions farther away from the public eye and the public trust. We succeed because of who we are, how we act, and what we say. As St. Francis of Assisi so eloquently stated:

Go forth and teach. Use words if necessary.

We're seen as teachers, guides, and exemplars. Thus, hypocrisy is a poison that can kill a speaker's reputation, most completely and irretrievably.

There was a Christian minister (and I use both words loosely) in Dallas, Texas who unknowingly exposed his true character and suffered the consequences for it. After he'd finished his sermon one Sunday (a sermon emphasizing the importance of love, compassion and acting charitably), the minister left the sanctuary and headed to the childcare area where he unleashed a tirade of angry, verbal abuse against his wife.

But he'd forgotten to turn off his microphone. So, while everyone was in the quiet of closing prayers in the "holy" sanctuary, his shocking, hateful language was heard by all — prompting his immediate firing. Perhaps this minister had never contemplated

Aristotle's assertion that the orator's personal character is "the most effective means of persuasion he possesses."

In *The Speaker's Industry Report*, Lilly Walters asked, "What things would you like to tell speakers, but are too polite or intimidated to say or ask?"

One meeting planner responded:

> **Be the same off stage as you are on stage. I've been around some highly touted humanitarian speakers who talked about their compassionate exploits, but they treated the catering staff like dirt! Their phoniness was so blatant, it was difficult after that to even introduce them to the audience who would only see their public face.**

It really pays to practice what you preach, and preach only what you practice. Count on this — people will be watching! I facilitate a two-day customer service-training course that encourages people not to lose their cool, not even when the situation seems to beg for it. The particular terminology used is this admonition — "Don't get hooked." (When a fish gets hooked, only the fisherman wins!)

I once went to pick up some lunches for myself and my co-workers at Baja Fresh, my favorite fast-food Mexican restaurant. Because time was short, we'd faxed in our order. When I got there, it was very crowded. *Finally*, getting to the front, I asked for my food.

"We don't have your order. You'll have to check our other restaurant in town."

"Would you be willing to check to see if the fax went there?"

Her brusque reply insulted me: "We're really busy right now, so you'll just have to wait!"

As I watched her complete a few more orders, my heart began pounding as my frustration mounted. This was unacceptable! I thought, "I've had enough!"

I was on the verge of unleashing verbiage that my own daughters have never witnessed. (OK… rarely witnessed.)

But I warned myself, "Don't get hooked! Don't get hooked!"

Just then, a cashier approached me and informed me that they had just called, and my order had in fact been sent to the other location.

She offered apologies for the error and suggested, "If you can drive over there, your order will be waiting for you. And here is a discount voucher for 25% off for your inconvenience. Again, we're sorry."

I said that was fine and thanked them for their help.

As I was leaving, I heard my name being called. I turned around and there stood Steve, one of the vice-presidents of our company.

"I was standing back there in the corner and heard everything you said," he shared. "I just wanted to see if you'd get *hooked*. Congratulations, you kept your cool!"

I couldn't believe it! Steve had been in that course with me four years earlier! He remembered! And he was still watching my actions!

People don't forget these kinds of things because we speakers are issuing the challenges, promoting the truths, and they want to see if we live what we talk.

When they observe you off the stage, they're going to be asking themselves "Was it just lip service?" or "Does he or she really live this?" I remember thinking when I left Baja Fresh how glad I was that I'd kept my cool and passed a test that I'd not even been aware I was taking. Someone was there, waiting to see if I was a hypocrite.

I'd rather see a sermon than hear one any day;
I'd rather one should walk with me than merely tell the way
The eye's a better pupil and more willing than the ear,
Fine counsel is confusing, but example's always clear...

—from poem *Sermons We See,* by Edgar Guest

Chapter Six

Fueling the Fire

The past chapter warned us — **DON'T EXTINGUISH YOUR FIRE!**

This chapter encourages us — **FUEL YOUR FIRE!**

I've been speaking to audiences for over 30 years. I can vividly recall the "early days" when I witnessed *unspeakable* horrors. I actually saw audience members yawning, checking their watches, and even nodding!

OUCH!

There are few experiences in life more humbling than to be baring your soul to the throngs, only to be ignored in return. Thus, I made a resolute pact with myself three decades ago:

I will not be a boring speaker!
(My guess is that everyone who bought this book probably feels the same way.)

Thus, I graciously hand over the following "fuels." These are the logs tossed on a fire that not only keep it burning, but send the flames higher and higher. These "logs for the fire" will create warmth and light…

…and captivation!

So, let's toss on a few logs and enjoy the dancing flames!

1. PITCH

It has been suggested that speakers have a range of twenty-four musical notes, including sharps and flats. Most speakers rarely use more than eight. Some speakers use only two or three notes, and some only one — the infamous, sleep-inducing monotone.

Just imagine how much that hinders the music that we could be playing! Imagine a symphony that was composed entirely of those eight notes. That piece would have the crowd rising to its feet… and heading for the exits! It is captivating when we use our full range of notes in speaking, because it's so rarely done.

When you explore that vocal range, taking your voices lower and higher, it helps build that dramatic tension. You can change pitch to accentuate points you feel strongest about. And when you quote dialogue, differently pitched voices enliven the conversation. And don't forget the effectiveness of a different pitch to state the passion statement in your speech.

It takes practice to both properly and credibly extend your vocal range higher and lower. These explorations will feel awkward at first, but they will begin to feel more and more natural to you and, more importantly, to your audiences. Start practicing — in the shower or in the tub, like Sir Winston.

2. RATE

What's too fast? Too slow? When I do presentation skills workshops, I ask, "Do you think that most speakers tend to speak too quickly or too slowly?"

The answer is invariably, "Too quickly." Then I ask why they think speakers rush their presentations. The class members attribute it to nervousness and the desire to just get it over with so they can sit down.

One of the keys to professionalism and captivation is to **never rush** the delivery. Now, it's true that the adrenaline rush experienced in speaking is equaled by only one other activity that humans enjoy. Imagine your partner saying afterwards, "I just wanted to get it over with as soon as possible."

Not very enchanting or captivating…right?

Don't rush things that are meant to be memorable (I'm back to talking about speaking now). Slow it down so the audience knows you are delivering something important:

Speakingtoofastunderminesalloftheotherqualitiesofanexcellentspeech.

See what I mean? So, vary the pace. Savor your words. Go slower than normal, then a little faster than normal, then at a mid-range rate. If you can constantly be shifting through four or five different speeds, it will immensely benefit your delivery.

3. PAUSE

Pause. You are having a dialogue with the audience when you say something profound or ask them a question. Give them time to think before you continue.

—Patricia Fripp

I love…the pause. It's my favorite oratory technique and, I believe, the most powerful tool in speaking! But it's too rarely practiced and used. Why is that?

Speakers tell me:
> "I'm too nervous!"
> "I'm supposed to be the one in charge."
> "Pauses lead to an awkward silence in the room."
> "They will think I lost my place."

If there is a sense of awkwardness, don't let it affect you. Let the audience be stimulated by it. Another way to view awkwardness is that it's a type of captivation. People won't sleep through it, and it creates a bit of tension and suspense in the room.

Another benefit of the pause is that, YES, it does give us time to think — and to read the crowd's reaction. Speakers who don't use the pause have yet to discover its power!

Too often speakers use distracting audible pauses, such as "um's" and "er's." These presenters are also the ones who are often caught off guard about what to say next. Pausing between profundities and questions gives both the speaker and the audience time to think. Let your points sink in, especially your passion statements. I can think of no more powerful example of "the pause" than in Churchill's famous "chicken" speech.

This was a speech he gave to Parliament after England had survived assault after assault by the Luftwaffe. Wanting to bolster his country's morale, he revealed the Vichy French government's earlier prediction upon England's entry into the war:

"Within two weeks, Germany will wring England's neck like a chicken."
(He paused, intently looking at his audience —)

"..........Some chicken!"

(Cheers, shouts, applause — and when that settled down —)

".........Some neck!"

Parliament members arose and roared, full of pride and patriotism!

Echoes resounded throughout the halls…

…and the world!

I got a chill just writing this.

But imagine the loss of effectiveness if he had not so dramatically employed the pause. Take the Churchill quote and read it aloud without the pauses. Then…read it again… including the pauses. See if that second reading doesn't give you goose bumps, or as they say in Britain — "goose pimples."

Comedy, too, is dependent upon captivating pauses:

It's not so much knowing when to speak, as when to pause.

—Jack Benny

And in music as well:

> **The notes I handle no better than many pianists. But the pauses between the notes — ah, that is where the art resides!**
>
> **—Arthur Schnabel**

So…let's add this powerful fuel to our arsenal…

And…watch…the…flames…rise!

4. VOLUME

Of all the books, videos and tapes I've explored on presentation skills, I've never heard the method that I personally use regarding volume as a captivator in a speech. My approach is simply called "The Ten-X Theory." It works this way. When I go before an audience, I estimate the number of people in the room. I then multiply that number by ten, and that's how many people I address. If there's a group of ten, my volume range is geared to address one hundred.

This is easier said than done, because our volume is "programmed." We are all raised with volume "governors"—

"Keep your voice down!"

"You don't have to shout!"

"Use your indoor voice!"

Give some thought to your speaking voice and your speaking venue. Observe how dinner party volume levels differ from those used at a baseball game. You'll need to override your natural volume governor. (This takes practice.) Charles Spurgeon regularly spoke to audiences of ten thousand without a microphone, and he once addressed a multitude of 23,634 *without any* mechanical amplification!

Another advantage to utilizing The Ten-X Theory is that once you've got your volume correct and you're on fire at that level, you can vary it and still be heard. Sometimes, you can even bring it down to a captivating whisper. Adjust your volume up and down according to what you're attempting to achieve, and the audience will follow the flow. But *always* try to increase your volume when you're revealing the passion statement. And always "play" to the back of the room. As an accomplished speaker once advised me:

> **The man sitting in the corner farthest from you has poor hearing, and uses a hearing aid. Today, he left it at home. So speak loudly enough for him to understand you!**

5. GRAMMAR

> **Think as wise men do, but speak as the common people do.**
>
> **—Aristotle**

I confess that I am of two minds about grammar. On the one hand, I believe our speeches should be grammatically sound. On the other, I don't want grammar to become the enemy of captivating language.

Admittedly, there are those few people who will immediately discount a speaker, who will disconnect from that orator, if his or her usage is not rigidly proper. They look for dangling modifiers, split infinitives, and the like. But most people look for connection. They may discount speakers who overly adhere to grammatical rules. Thus, I strive for a complementary relationship — a healthy, give-and-take marriage.

There are times when you'll choose to intentionally use bad grammar — when your love of language supersedes your desire to be a polished grammarian. For example, just to rid yourself of a dangling preposition, you wouldn't change:

"I had to find out what was up"

to

"I had to find out that which up was."

You want the umpire to shout,

"Yer OUT!"

not

"I've determined that your attempt to steal second base was UNSUCCESSFUL!"

We have to balance grammatical correctness with creativity and power. Grammar is a dynamic structure that changes to meet the needs of a living, evolving language. Grammar is intended to support and preserve the richness of communication. Its primary purpose is to ensure clarity, nothing more.

We don't want to tell someone who asks how the speech went, "Well, most of them fell asleep on me, but it certainly was grammatically correct." We want to say, "I felt really connected with them!"

I suggest that you study grammar, but don't become a slave to it. Research potential problem areas that you might have. The more you know about good grammar, the better you'll also understand when there's a situation in which you may choose *not* to utilize it.

We all come from the factory wired for language. By the time we know what it is, we've got it. Toddlers don't think about language; they just talk. Grammar is a later addition, an ever-evolving set of rules for using words in ways that we can agree on. But the laws of grammar come and go. English today isn't what it was a hundred years ago, and it's not what it will be a hundred years

from now. We make up rules when we need them, and discard them when we don't. Then when do we need them? When our wires get crossed and we fail to understand one another.

—From Patricia T. O'Conner's excellent book on grammar, *Woe Is I.*

6. QUESTIONS

Why are questions so powerful?

Have you considered the benefits of asking for audience responses?

How do questions encourage dialogue and discourage lecture?

I recall listening to a speaker who began her presentation asking, "How old would you be if you didn't know how old you are?"

This inspired laughter and discussion in the group...

"Does that mean how old do I feel?"

"How old do I look?"

It made an immediate connection and it led into the point of her talk.

Asking questions is also a good opportunity to start off with some humor:

"How many people are in the wrong place?"

"How many wish they were in the wrong place?"

"How many care where they are?"

"How many wish I would stop asking questions?"

People will laugh, and you'll see hands raised after each question. This provides both spark and a change of pace.

You do have to be careful, however, when you're asking rhetorical questions because some people won't pick up on the fact that they are rhetorical. It's not that I don't love to get responses from the group. I frequently interact with audiences. But there are times in a speech when you don't want people shouting out answers. It can undermine a dramatic or inspirational point in your speech. You can't ignore that raised hand or that shout. I effectively set up rhetorical questions by letting the audience know in various phrasings that no verbal response is expected. I'll say…

"Let me just ask you a few rhetorical questions…"
> or

"I want you just to think about possible answers to this question…"
> or

"There's no need to respond to this, but why would…"

These pretty much guarantee that you won't be faced with the awkwardness of someone speaking up from the audience when you'd rather them not.

Why don't more speakers use this magical device that shows respect?

Why do teachers rarely use questions, except on tests?

Will you consider asking more questions in your presentations?

Can you think of a better way to involve others?

7. QUOTES

Quotes are powerful captivators and credibility-builders. (Notice how many I use in this book). They show respect for other's thoughts. Whenever possible, quote people in the audience, as it delights and honors them.

If you're speaking to a company, quote its leaders. Sure, you could quote Jack Welch and other famous CEO's, but why not the locals? It makes everything more specific and intimate. (And it doesn't hurt to know that it's the company leaders who have a say in whether you're invited back to speak again.) If you know there's a new executive or associate at the company, quote them. Get them to stand, and initiate applause for them. Honor them. There are many, many ways to incorporate quotes effectively.

A company I worked for sponsored a "Bring Your Child To Work Day," as many organizations have done. I invited my older daughter, Alexandra. On that particular day, I was facilitating the Presentation Skills Workshop for seven executives in finance. These managers had three months to prepare presentations that each would be giving in the afternoon session. I made it clear to Alexandra, of course, that she wasn't expected to present one with such short notice. She said she'd like to, if she could go last.

During each speaker's afternoon presentation, I observed Alexandra was taking copious notes. After everyone had finished, it was time for Alexandra's presentation. What she did was really remarkable! As her father, I couldn't have been more proud.

She had taken notes on all of the other speakers' topics. Then she demonstrated how the power of the Internet could enhance each of their topics. And she quoted the speakers:

> Today we heard Maria discuss her keen interest in the country of Morocco. She said, "Morocco is a magical place!" Well, it's exciting to know that you can go to this Internet site (and she mentioned the site) and listen to Moroccan music as you're doing your research.

She went from one speaker to the next, remembering their topics and quoting them.

Everyone was excited and loved that their interests were being recapped! They were ecstatic that *their words* were quoted. Why? Because *their words* were honored! They gave Alexandra a tremendous round of applause.

They loved her words, because her words were their words!

Quoting others is a powerful fuel for your "fires."

I strongly suggest memorizing your twenty favorite quotes. It's always better not to have to read them from your notes. After all, if they've really had an impact on you, wouldn't you know them by heart?

This is what the audience is thinking.

And you can "quote me" on that!

8. ENUNCIATE

Of all the flammable fuels we're going to study, enunciation has been my number one nemesis — my biggest challenge. I've never fully understood some of the difficulties others experience with such things as volume or pauses, but I think I can empathize when it comes to this one. I've had the hardest time with enunciation.

I was born and raised in North Carolina, and have a distinct Southern accent. Shortly after college, I moved from North Carolina to Boston where I got my first speaking job. Boy, did I "catch it" there! It must have been during Jimmy Carter's administration because I kept hearing things about being a "peanut farmer." However, it wasn't just my accent.

It was also my enunciation of words. From Boston, I moved to London. A Southern Yank! Caught a lot more flak! From London to Sydney. Same thing. And I've always found it interesting that people across the world could pick up that I had not only an American accent, but a Southern one as well. I finally learned that my accent is something I could never change. But I *could learn* to better enunciate my words. This would lessen the distraction that my accent might create for others.

There was a time, however, when I went to considerable lengths to rid myself of my, shall I say, "oratory Southerninity." When I was a minister in England, I spoke regularly to a large, British congregation. They never complained to me, but it was suggested by other leaders of the church that if I were to drop my Southern accent and acquire a more English elocution, it would give the entire church a boost. The intention was to minimize any existing anti-American sentiment the congregation or visitors might have had.

Heeding this advice, I tried to overcome my provenance. I really tried hard! I took lessons from RADA, the world-renowned Royal Academy of Dramatic Arts. A stately woman who was convinced that she would have me speaking the Queen's English "in no time at t'all" personally tutored me. (She'd successfully tutored Dick Van Dyke for the movie *Mary Poppins*.)

And so it began… I'd meet with her two nights a week, each time for an hour. *Very* expensive — but I figured it was well worth it.

Week after week of lessons soon became month after month. Nothing changed. And, believe me, I practiced. I did the homework. I progressed to the point where I could read the Queen's English pretty well. I couldn't speak it, though, particularly when I got excited. Every time I was in front of the congregation and "caught fire," I'd revert back to the "Land of Cotton" — a source of considerable amusement to the brethren.

I continued to press. Stiff upper lip and all that. It was "tally ho" until the night I came to tutoring and my teacher told me, "This evening's lesson will be our last."

"No, no, no! We're just getting it going here. I've got the money. I'm paying you on time!"

"No, that's not the point. James, I'm afraid it's a waste of *your money* and a waste of *my time*."

Ooooh... I was so humbled! She was getting paid a *lot* of money to do this with me, and she could no longer continue with a clear conscience — it just wasn't working. I, thus, sadly, (really – *gladly*) took my leave of the Queen's English. That was the last time I tried to change my accent.

Years later, in a three-day workshop in San Diego, I met an extraordinary man named Larry. His passion was accents. When I related this story to him, he told me that deep down, I didn't really want to lose my accent — my regional dialect — nor should I. He called it my "voice fingerprint." I liked that. And he was right. I probably never should have tried to lose my accent because it's really an essential part of who I am.

I used to get offended when people would make fun and try to imitate it. My friend Daniel once told me that it was funny how sensitive I was about my accent, while Jeff Foxworthy has made millions of dollars exploiting his.

I started thinking about that comment, did a little research, and discovered something interesting. When Foxworthy first started performing in New York, the advice he got, coincidentally, was to take lessons to get rid of *his* Southern accent as well. New Yorkers were always kidding him about being nothing but an "ol' redneck from Georgia." Well, that "ol' redneck" is the top-selling comedy artist in recording history. His first CD sold more than three million copies! He's published ten best-selling books, and has starred in numerous television specials.

Jeff Foxworthy remained who he was. He kept his accent as part of his uniqueness, and it paid off. If he'd lost it, what else might he have lost? It's also worth noting that his style is not one of boasting and bragging. He is poking fun at his culture, his habits, his family, and his accent. That kind of fire burns brightly!

Some people's prejudices will make them disconnect when they hear an accent. If you can find ways to circumvent this, it will contribute greatly to your success. In *Smart Speaking*, by Laurie Schloff and Marcia Yudkin, the practice of "plosives" is introduced. I won't go into detail, but it's the practice of pronouncing two conjoined consonants as a method of speaking more clearly.

The best and most complete audio workshop that I've encountered on diction, elocution, correction of foreign accents, and local dialects is Zoller's *Speaking Effective English*. This two-tape audio delves deeply into the science of speech. It includes numerous exercises to alleviate problems with vowel sounds, diphthongs, consonants, etc. It even has pauses that allow time for the listener to practice aloud with the tape.

If you want to speak more clearly, you may also wish to consider emulating Demosthenes. In ancient Greece, Demosthenes was the greatest orator in an era of exceptional oratory. As a child, he heard the magic of the spoken word and decided that speaking was his destiny. But he had one big problem. Demosthenes was born with a speech impediment that greatly affected both his volume and enunciation. As I've mentioned earlier, we are not born with talent; talent is developed through the hard work of practice.

And work hard he did. Demosthenes would go to the beach. To work on his volume, he would stand on the rocks and practice speaking, shouting against the sound of crashing surf. He'd also pick up small pebbles and put them in his mouth to practice enunciating his words. By intentionally adding further impediments to his inherent one, with passionate practice, he was victorious.

I often imagine what he looked like, standing proudly, shouting at the waves.

And sometimes, when I am alone at a beach where waves are crashing, I hear the ghost of Demosthenes…and I'm inspired.

9. STATISTICS

65 percent of all audience members appreciate statistics. 100 percent of people will show their appreciation 50 percent of the time by evaluating 95 percent of your presentations at an average 8.9 on a 1-10 scale. (Sorry, I couldn't resist.) Seriously, effective use of statistics really appeals to those "thinkers" in the audience. They want facts, figures, and precision.

When you use statistics, be graphically dramatic and creative, and always give your sources when it will lend credibility. Audience retention is augmented when you accompany statistics with clear, uncomplicated visuals. Statistics have no meaning without interpretation. When interpreted well, a few dramatic numbers can be invaluable.

If you've got a nice figure, flaunt it!

—*Taking Center Stage*, by Gottesman and Mauro

I won over an audience of information technologists by employing a statistical comparison that I discovered on the Internet. I call it my "Jock vs. Nerd Stat Story."

Here are the statistical innards of the story:
* Michael Jordan — the "semi-retired" Michael Jordan, that is — now makes $40 million a year in endorsements.

* That translates into $178,000 per day.

* If he goes to see a movie, it'll cost him $8.00, but he'll make $18,550 while watching it!

* If someone were to hand him his salary, dollar by dollar, they would have to do so at the rate of $2.00 every second.

* This year, he'll make more than twice as much as all past U.S. Presidents, for *all* of their terms combined.

* Amazing! However, if Jordan saves 100% of his income for the next 450 years, he'll still have *less* than Bill Gates (the "nerd") has today!

I know very little about what information technologists do for a living, but I do know that in a "jock vs. nerd" survey, most of them would fall more into the "nerdish" category. And when I ended that story with "Game over. Nerd wins!" something interesting happened — hands shot up around the room!

One participant initiated her first comments since our class had started.

"I *love* Bill Gates. He is responsible for putting computers in schools throughout our nation!"

Another member of the class commented, "I saw a TV special on Mr. Gates once. He had dirt under his fingernails because he does his *own* gardening!"

As others eagerly shared, classmates responded with "*ooh's*" and "*aah's.*"

I smiled, as I had just learned the power of audience-specific statistics.

10. PROPS

Props are so captivating, so effective, so connecting. In his book, *Do Not Go Naked into Your Next Presentation*, Ron Hoff discusses the importance of good props:

> **I've been trying to forget the O.J. Simpson trial, but one picture keeps developing itself over and over in my mind. It's defense attorney Johnny Cochran, delivering his summation to the jury. He's wearing a dark stocking cap, pulled down right over his head. The cap was a piece of prosecution evidence, but it didn't look very dangerous on Johnny. And the most compelling part of this picture is that it's locked in my brain forever. Images have a way of doing that. Never underestimate the power of a vivid image to make linkages into the mind that words alone simply cannot accomplish.**

Cochran's is a good example of prop-power. I've already related a number of instances when speakers used props with excellent effect. You've probably seen examples as well.

It's always fun when you use props that you can hand out to members of the audience.

My friend, Marda, gave a presentation entitled, *"Who Packs Your Parachute?"* in which, instead of simply thanking the audience for all the community service they'd done, she gave each audience member a little plastic paratrooper — something memorable for them. Great fuel!

As mentioned earlier, I once used **nine** different props in a speech. Also, whenever I tell one of my signature stories — the Nordstrom Story — I actually hold up the ratty old green shirt I'm talking about, so the audience can see it. When I share about my phone call to my wife, I actually speak into my cell phone. When I mention that I was lacking cash for a transaction, I pull out my wallet from my back pocket and rummage through it with a sad look on my face. I don't just tell about the tie I bought, I wear it and flaunt it.

This is the captivating power of props, and they are especially essential in meeting the needs of visual and kinesthetic learners in your audience. (More on the different styles of learners will be discussed later in this chapter).

11. HUMOR

I wait until I've opened a mouth wide with laughter... Then I pour a dose of truth down it.

—Charles Spurgeon

Well said. The proper use of humor in your speeches has effects well beyond its entertainment value. It loosens up the crowd, and opens them up to your message. I have my own "humor file" of about two hundred pages. It contains humorous stories I've heard and jokes I've been told or have seen on television, in newspapers, magazines, and e-mails. I read maybe a book each month on humor, constantly looking for gems. Whenever I use one of the jokes from my file, I go back in the book and write down where I used it, for whom, and the response it received. Then, I might rework it, reword it and use it again later. I make it a point, though, to never build any speech around humor. I wait until the speech writing is completed, then look for a place where an appropriate joke or humorous story might "stack on."

[Humor] can soften controversy and relieve tension. It can get the audience's attention back if they're drifting. And, most importantly, it can make them like you. Everyone enjoys spending time with someone who has a sense of humor, and if the audience enjoys spending time with you, you'll have a much better chance of achieving your objective than if they don't.

...never apologize for a joke in any way. No "Stop me if you've heard this one" or "Indulge me for just a moment." No shrugging or other apologetic body language. If the joke is in the speech, you should already have determined that it's appropriate, relevant to the material, and worth telling."

—*Taking Center Stage,* by Gottesman and Mauro

So, please don't stop me if you've heard this one. Find good comedy material, develop it, and practice it. Go to comedy clubs and watch stand-up on television. Examine how jokes are told well. Look for timing, pauses, facial expressions, body language, etc. Now, go put some smiles on some faces!

Laughter is the shortest distance between two people.

—Victor Borge

12. MOVEMENT

You don't have to be *Elvis!* You don't have to get up there and "*shake that thang.*" But neither do you have to stand behind the podium in a classical pose like *Venus de Milo*. The audience's eyes are dying for stimulation. Walk, stomp, go from one side of the stage to the other, turn your back to the audience, walk away and come back, jump, squat, lie down, run, stumble, trip and fall, go into the audience — anything, but stand still! Try using a lavaliere mike. Most speakers want a "fixed" mike so they can stay behind the podium. I know it's safer back there, but being safe works against being captivating.

One thing that got me out from behind the podium was learning about its history. Centuries ago, the podium, or lectern, was used in the church, and designed to separate the minister from the audience. These podiums were usually "raised" as a symbol of the difference between the exalted holy man and the sinners to whom he preached. This bothered me because the last thing I wanted was to be separated from the group because we're *all* "sinners." My purpose is to connect with them, not distance myself.

13. CALLBACKS

In the beginning is my end.
In the end is my beginning.

—T.S. Eliot

I only learned about the callback a few years ago by watching comedians. Let's say that a comedian has a thirty-minute set. He or she will tell a good joke or humorous story at the beginning, or perhaps at about the fifteen-minute mark. Then they'll refer back, or "callback," to that joke in their final words in the performance. This method serves to remind the audience of the earlier joke, tie the entire performance together, and get a second round of laughter from the original joke. Watch for this! Great stuff!

I've since noticed that some speakers do the same thing. In fact, it seems to be a hallmark of the more professional speakers. Callbacks can be used in motivational and inspirational speeches just as effectively as they can in comedy.

For example, when I speak on customer service, I open the speech with "*Thank you for allowing me the opportunity to serve you today.*" At first, the audience isn't sure where I'm heading, but I weave this statement into the body of the speech. It's there again when I reach the passion point:

"*Thank you for allowing me the opportunity to serve you today.*" I close with the very same statement, and its message has been woven throughout the presentation.

So… *Thank you for allowing me the opportunity to share this with you.*

In the beginning is my end
In my end is my beginning.

—T.S. Elliot

14. EDITING

Add for interest, comprehension and humor. Edit for boredom.

—Hermine Hilton

Imagine paying someone to print your speech and that you're being charged per word. You're going to want to considerably streamline it before you hand it over to the printer. Using this mind-set, please edit the following sentence, deleting unnecessary words:

Go over your first rough draft thoroughly to be sure to eliminate completely all of the unnecessary words and phrases that can weaken your entire message.

Here's what you could have eliminated:

Go over your [first rough] **draft** [thoroughly] **to** [be sure to] **eliminate** [completely all of the] **unnecessary words** [and phrases] **that** [can] **weaken your** [entire] **message**.

Same message…fewer words…more captivating.

Some sparks on the value of editing –

> **I am still editing my oldest, best stories. A look, a gesture, a word is emphasized differently. It is a process that is honed by presenting and getting feedback and then reworking. Enhancing the presentation by editing cannot be done in a vacuum intellectually.**
>
> **—Rosita Perez**

> **Alfred Hitchcock had some good advice for writers: "Drama is life with the dull bits cut out." When professional writers talk about editing, they use a phrase reminiscent of Medea: "Kill your babies." They mean even though you may be in love with an idea or a turn of phrase, if it does not serve the speech as a whole, it has to die.**
>
> **—*Taking Center Stage*, by Gottesman and Mauro**

I've had to remind myself time and time again of the above words throughout the writing, re-writing, and relentless editing of this book. Words, sentences, paragraphs, and even entire chapters were edited, "*killed*."

And I *loved* every message that was snipped.

15. WATER

Water — the ultimate fuel. It sounds pretty basic, but I notice a lot of speakers who've yet to learn that there's no substitute for water, whether you're speaking for thirty minutes or an hour, or running a two-day workshop. I see speakers who drink sodas, maybe because of that little energy burst from caffeine, or because they enjoy that refreshing fizz. But there's a price to pay! Belching into your microphone is *not* the way to make friends and influence people!

Coffee and tea are options for some of us — you get the caffeine without the carbonation. But these beverages are also diuretics, and you don't want to be frequently excusing yourself to use the restroom. Milk can create mucus in the throat, thus leading to the undesirable distraction of having to clear your throat. And the less said about booze, the better. You're not one of the passengers. You are the pilot. Enjoy your drinks after you've safely landed the plane.

So that leaves us with water — the only liquid fuel for speakers. I'll take several bottles of water and put them on the podium. (For me, that's what a podium is for: something stable on which to put your props, notes and water bottles. I rarely stand behind it to speak.) Also, a speaker once told me that it's best to keep your water at room temperature. Ice-cold water makes your vocal chords contract, which significantly limits your vocal range. If you don't bring your own water, arrive early enough to find unrefrigerated water, or take water out of the refrigerator and let it stand for a while before you speak.

16. SMILE

Radiate the flame. Smile! This is the most powerful non-verbal gesture. You can smile even in the most serious speech. There's always room for it. And it invariably ignites the connection and warms the crowd. Smiling has never come as natural to me as it has for many other speakers. I've really had to work on it. I'm not sure why. Maybe it's my intensity, especially when I'm at my passion statement, that almost precludes thoughts of smiling.

So, I've really had to focus on it. One thing I've done, which has been very effective for me, is to pick out a friend in the audience and have him or her watch me for my smile. I ask her to keep a tally of how many times I smile during my speech. I have her jot down the places in my speech when I smiled, how long it lasted, and note how the audience reacted. I also watch my videos to see if my smile looks forced or natural, timely or untimely.

By smiling, you are inviting the audience to participate in your joy.

Smiles beget smiles in return.

Practice that smile. *Come on*, right here and now. That's it! Smile!
…The powerful smile!
…It warms the crowd.
…It quenches the nay-sayers.
…It ignites the connection.
…It radiates the flame!

17. EYE CONTACT

I'm looking you directly in the eye as I discuss this topic — eye contact.

The most appalling guidelines I've found regarding any aspect of speaking relate to this skill. In nine out of the fifty books on public speaking I read prior to writing this book, it was advised that if you are nervous about making eye contact with people in the audience, you should focus your vision at the back of the room, *over the heads* of the audience.

That this advice is still given simply astounds me! Sure, it would help you with nervousness, but you'll also wind up completely disconnecting yourself from the group. All it takes is *one* minute — sixty seconds — for this to happen. It won't matter how great your message is or how big your smile is. Volume, pauses, non-verbals — *none* of this matters — if you're not making eye contact. Work on nervousness some other way — (better preparation, perhaps?)

In my presentation skills workshop, everybody learns the importance of looking at each person in the room and giving them two to five seconds of eye contact. If the group is 75-100 people, I teach speakers to mentally divide the audience into groups of five, and then focus on one person in each small group. Every time they return to that group of five, they choose someone else with whom to connect.

If the group is larger, purposely focus on the front rows, making personal eye contact. Then divide the rest of the audience, first in half, and then into groups of five or ten, and focus on someone in each group. These are ideas you'll find in most publications.

But here are some secrets to maximize eye contact:

- Be sure to remain unpredictable. If not, eye contact becomes stilted and superficial, thus, losing the intended impact. I've seen trainers working with groups as small as twelve seated around a table who will, to make sure that everyone is getting some eye contact, go right around the table from one person to the next, in either a clockwise or counter-clockwise direction. This certainly ensures that everyone is included, but the group soon figures out your modus operandi. You'll wind up seeing people acting unnaturally, getting quiet as you get near them, preparing themselves for your gaze. As soon as you pass, there's that sigh of relief, and they're disconnecting, until you get back around again. It's too much like hiding from the prison searchlight. Too predictable. To avoid this, look continuously at different areas of the room: back to front, right to left, front to right, etc. Just scatter it, and keep in mind that your intent is to involve everyone in the room.

- Moreover, contrary to popular advice, I don't believe it's a good idea to avoid making eye contact with negative or hostile audience members (again, my theory: **No Bad Audiences**). I might even give them *extra* eye contact. After all, I probably met them as they came in the room. Perhaps I interviewed them, trying to find ways to compliment them — just as I do with everyone else.

- Attempt to give each audience member as much eye contact as they desire. Yes, this takes some skill and a lot of practice, but it can be so rewarding and validating. Some people are able to indefinitely sustain eye contact with you, and enjoy it. Others, for reasons of their own, can't handle more than three seconds before they become very uncomfortable and look away. Turn *your* eyes away *first*, rather than making them break that contact. Your goal is to alleviate discomfort and to invite everyone to be involved and attentive.

I once attended a two-day presentation skills seminar hosted by a company called Communispond. The instructor told us that, when making eye contact, we should always focus on someone, and never speak while scanning the room. They called scanning "aerosol spraying." The idea was to speak your thoughts *directly to* people. I was a bit dubious at first, but then I got proof. They videotaped me speaking before and after I'd practiced what they preached, and it *did* make a difference in my presentation. The video didn't lie.

"Here's lookin' at ya!"

18. SPONTANEITY

It usually takes me more than three weeks to prepare a good impromptu speech.

—Mark Twain

In the speaking world, it has been said that spontaneity is "an endless combination of rehearsed possibilities." What we love to think of as "spur-of-the-moment" is most often that which has been practiced. Excellent, crowd-pleasing speakers have words-at-the-ready for all sorts of unrehearsed incidents and situations. It could be something as simple as a plate dropping when you're in the middle of a speech, or an electrical outage, or a fire alarm sounding.

Now, I'm not going to give you possible responses to such occurrences. That, after all, would be giving you my rehearsed spontaneities. The secret is for you to imagine these situations occurring, and rehearse your own "ad-libs." You can also get ideas from other speakers and comics who are good at being "spontaneous." There are also many books on the market that are full of off-the-wall quips that may be helpful.

The key is to *sound* unrehearsed, not *be* unrehearsed. I was at a three-day seminar in which the leader told a lot of stories, but the stories weren't tight. They weren't edited or streamlined. Consequently, the stories dragged on longer than necessary. Statements were made, such as, "Oh, I forgot to say this" or "Oh, I need to mention this first." It was obvious that time had not been spent to polish these stories.

As I sat there, disappointed with her lack of preparation, the leader revealed her philosophy of spontaneity:

> Don't ever rehearse your stories in order to ensure they will appear natural. It's okay to have "um's" and "ah's" because otherwise, you will sound staged and rehearsed.

This is a philosophy worth considering. We certainly don't want to sound *so* polished that the audience starts wondering how many times we've told that story before. Yet, without the practice, those stories were so disjointed and loosely woven that they lacked maximum punch. There's a fine line between being well-rehearsed and over-rehearsed. My advice is to rehearse to the point where it appears unrehearsed.

19. RECOVERY

The mind is a wonderful thing. It starts to work the minute you are born and never stops until you get up to speak in public.

—John Mason Brown

Our ultimate fear:

What if I get up there, and my mind just goes totally blank?

Memory can desert you when you can least afford it. And few nightmares are as chilling as the thought of that flame sputtering and flickering out!

Let's come up with a couple of strategies to help insure against this. And if it still happens, let's discuss ways to confidently handle the situation.

First of all, always have notes. You don't have to read them. You don't have to refer to them. But have them with you, just in case.

I remember the first major speech I gave. I was in my early twenties when I was invited to speak before 3000 people in the old Boston Garden. My speech was twenty color-coded, highlighted, handwritten pages long. I'd practiced on my own about two dozen times, then practiced in front of a video recorder ten times. Watched, tightened, watched, changed a phrase, watched, tried new physical gestures, etc.

When it came time for the speech, I remember walking out and setting my lengthy notes on the podium. Page one was staring at me. Then I began…

After the close, I went to grab my notes and noticed I was *still looking* at page one. I'd never referred to the notes — never even turned the first page! Why did I have those twenty pages? Just in case. If I'd lost my train of thought at any time during that speech, I could have quickly recovered.

Early in his career, Winston Churchill was to address Parliament. He got up without notes, looked around, and started to speak. After a few minutes, he abruptly stopped and just stared at his audience. His mind had blanked. After what seemed an uncomfortable eternity, he sat down and put his head in his hands, utterly humiliated. He vowed *never, never, never* again. After that, he was *never* without notes.

Another recovery strategy is to ask the audience to help you when you've drawn a blank. Most people are eager to help you, especially if you've already made a connection with them. You can do this in a "down home" informal way –

"What was I just saying?"

"What point was I just making?"

Use a humorous line afterwards:

"You know, they say that when you get older, your memory is the second thing to go...what's the first?"

Or say something like:

"Okay, it's time for a test to see how well you are listening. What was the last point I was making?"

After you're told, say:

"Thank you! You've just passed the test."

You might even include:

"Thank you for passing that test because I had *no clue* where I was."

It gets them laughing.

If your mind goes blank, Neil Poindexter advises to pause and ask:

"What questions do you have at this point?"

(This is more for a training session, of course.) Turn it over to the audience. If someone does ask a question, then you're back on track. If no one does, at least you gain credit for asking, and it gives you precious time to either remember where you were or to transition into your next point.

These are just a few tips on graceful recoveries. You'll probably come up with a number of your own, and …and…Oh my gosh!

(…My mind just totally blanked!)

20. DRESS

I came in to work one Tuesday morning and my boss quickly approached me and said, "James, I need to ask you to do a major favor for me. It's one of the biggest favors I've ever asked."

"Of course. I'd be willing to do anything for you…because *bonus time* is right around the corner."

She chuckled and explained that she needed to be in downtown Los Angeles, where there was a major luncheon scheduled that day. It was a $100 per plate function for the National Association of Women Business Owners. The CEO of our company was speaking, and the Mayor of Los Angeles would be in attendance as well. She was supposed to be there at one of the tables, but was not able to make it. It was important that there be no empty seats.

"I'll do it," I promptly declared.

She thanked me, and added, "James, you need to dress your absolute best. I'm really going to ask that you put on your best suit for this."

She then told me that I had to head to Los Angeles immediately because it was going to take time to get there and I had to be there early. I reassured her, saying that I would indeed not embarrass her in any way and that I would certainly wear my very best suit. (What I didn't tell her was that I had only *one* suit at the time, so it wouldn't be difficult to find my *best* one.)

On the way home to quickly change into this *best* and *only* suit, I shockingly remembered that it was at the cleaners being altered! I quickly drove to the cleaners and asked them for my suit, and they calmly told me it had been sent out to be altered. I hadn't realized that the alterations weren't done in-house, and this put me in a real bind. There was no way I could get it in time. Somehow, I had to get into a suit — and get into one *fast*. After rushing home and tearing through my closet, I was astonished to find I had a second suit. Sort of.

I hadn't thought of this garment as my suit for a very long time. Someone had given it to me back in 1982, almost twenty years *and ninety pounds ago!* But I had no other option. My other suit wasn't available. There was no time to run into town and grab one off the rack. Losing ninety pounds in twenty-five minutes seemed less than feasible. Yet, I was determined! This suit would suit me, one way or another.

The coat fit snugly, almost clownishly, but was a showpiece of sartorial craft compared to the pants. After a struggle, I finally got them over my hips. Not only could I neither fasten the snap nor button them, but the zipper couldn't be pulled up more than a quarter of an inch! You can imagine my panic at this point, thinking that there was no way I could go to a fancy luncheon like this. But I had to be there, so I calmed down and tried to figure out a way to make those pants fit. I had to call on my ingenuity.

The only thing I could think to do was take a pair of scissors and cut a "V" out of the waistband at the back. This would make some extra space and I figured that the coat would cover the notch anyway. When I tried on the trousers again, the zipper now went up just one inch! *Better*, but not there yet. About four inches to go! So, I took off the pants and cut out two more "V's" out of the back. The zipper came up another inch.

Snip, snip…Four more "V's."

Geometries expanded, as did the waistband.

When I'd finished, the floor was littered with small, black "V's." I had cut them out along the whole waistband, at every place except the belt loops. And it worked! I was now zippered, buttoned, belted, and on my way to represent my company at a function in downtown Los Angeles — feeling like Jethro Bodine of The Beverly Hillbillies.

I'll never forget how anxious I felt walking into that room of two thousand guests, hoping to inconspicuously blend into the crowd. It was, of course, not to be. I was noticed, but, oddly enough, not the way I'd feared. Ironically, people actually complimented me, saying, "You look really sharp today, James."

Whew! If they'd only known the truth about my precariously designed outfit! Had the least thing gone wrong — if I'd had to bend over for any reason — I might have exploded from those pants and been left standing in my skivvies! I spent the rest of the luncheon praying that no one would ask us to take off our coats. Thankfully, nobody did. I'd gotten away with one this time.

I'd always been a casual sort of guy. Image was never something I cared about very much. I think this comes from my strong belief that people are who they are on the inside, and how you look on the outside is not nearly as important. Although this is still, and will always be, my conviction, the truth is that when you get up to speak or do a presentation, people *are* judging you before you've even opened your mouth.

I now realized that I'd been very silly, even reckless, with my image. I had only one eight-year-old suit and it had a small tear in the sleeve of the coat, and here I was, speaking in front of groups all over the country.

The very next day after the luncheon, I went to The Men's Wearhouse and bought some nice clothing for the first time in many years — clothes that gave me a great deal more confidence when I got up to speak in front of a group — clothes that undoubtedly presented a much better image…

…and those *designer* suit-pants?

They're now a **wonderful** comedy prop!

21. IMPACT

Words represent your intellect. The sound, gesture and movement represent your feelings.

—Patricia Fripp

The powerful fuel of a message's impact is comprised of three parts:
1. words
2. tone of voice
3. non-verbals

What percentage of your entire speech's impact would you assign to the actual words? What about to your tone of voice? To the non-verbals? I've asked this of audiences. Of course, results varied, but very many people give a high percentage to the words of a message, most crowds as high as 50%.

In his extensive study, UCLA Professor Dr. Mehrabian provides these surprising results:

Words: 7%
Tone of Voice: 38%
Non-verbals: 55%

Is this anywhere near your estimation? Isn't it incredible that words could count for so little in the total message? Common sense seems to tell us otherwise.

We've heard —

> **By thy words, shalt thou be judged, and by thy words, condemned.**
>
> —**Matthew 12:37**
> **King James Version**

The importance of words is also reflected in the following quotes:

> **The difference between the almost right word and the right word 'tis the difference between the lightning bug and the lightning.**
>
> —**Mark Twain**

> **The original transcript for *The Power of Positive Thinking* was initially turned down; he (Dr. Peale) was really depressed about that, and threw it in the wastebasket. His wife, Ruth, took it out and brought it to a new publisher. This publisher looked at the work, then titled, *The Power of Positive Faith*, and said, "What keeps coming up here is the power of positive thinking; that should be the title of the book." The rest is history.**
>
> —**Les Brown**

This aforementioned book is perhaps the single most successful publication, other than the Bible. It's been translated into forty-two languages and has sold over 20 million copies. Why, therefore, the relative significance of words in the above examples? Ah, but Twain and Peale were writers, and thus, messengers from the written realms. Artists of the word are capable of conveying feelings, moods, tones, and even non-verbals, by the way they deliver messages. That's why writing is an art.

But we are speakers, and thus, have the liberty and responsibility not only to *express words*, but also to *fluctuate tone of voice*, and to *display non-verbals*.

Remember: professional words are only 7% of a professional delivery. Far too many speakers spend far too much time on the script of a speech. When they do rehearse, they rehearse the words, but not the presentation that makes those words both come to life and blaze into flames. Speak with conviction!

Picture someone with a deadpan monotone doing a serious reading of Martin Luther King, Jr.'s *I Have a Dream* speech. Would anyone *dream*, or would they simply *sleep?* It's *how the words are said* that makes all the difference.

I once demonstrated this difference between words and tone of voice to my daughters when they were seven and five. I was trying to explain apologies. I told them that when I demanded that they apologize, *how* they said the word "sorry" made all the difference. I proposed that an angry, or sulking, or convictionless "sorry" didn't really count. The word was right, but the tone of voice belied it.

We have an adorable little dog, Sheeka. I asked my daughters, "When we call Sheeka, and she comes to us happy and wagging her tail, do you think she knows and understands the words, or is she just responding to the tone of our voices?"

Both my children said they thought Sheeka knew the words. (Dogs are magically and wonderfully human, especially to young children.) Well, I knew I had to burst their bubble. I called Sheeka. My daughters watched intently.

Sheeka came up, wagging her tail as always, and I said in a happy, cooing, loving voice, "Now, Sheeka. Tomorrow I'm going to run over you in the car — Yes, I *am!* Yes, I *am!* And after I run over you, I'm going to go back and forth and *flatten* you like a *pancake*. Yes, I *am!*"

Naturally, Sheeka was licking me and wagging her tail the whole time. My daughters were in shock and disbelief at this revelation. I said, "I hated to do that, but see, Sheeka doesn't know the words. She only knows the *tone of voice*. So when you apologize, girls, *how you say it* makes a big difference."

So we have the words, our fluctuating tones, and lastly, the non-verbals, which constitute the greatest percentage of a message's impact. These, of course, are things like stance, hand gestures, body language, facial expressions — even pauses and timing are non-verbals.

I facilitated a class in California and was talking about the importance of non-verbals when a woman raised her hand and, as if she'd just solved a great mystery, exclaimed, "This explains it! This explains it!"

"What?"

"This study explains something I've never been able to understand."

"And what's that?"

"I love the opera. I just love it! I go to Los Angeles every weekend I can during opera season. In one evening, I'm happy, I'm sad, I laugh, I cry. I even feel *enormous* passion and sorrow."

Then she paused and continued, "And...I don't speak one word of Italian!"

Not understanding a word, amazingly she was still able to experience the *full essence* of an opera by *watching* and *listening!*

Perhaps the best example of the powerful propellant of non-verbals is *Blue Man Group*, one of the nation's hottest shows. You may have seen these men with blue-painted skin in some television commercials. I was privileged to attend their mesmerizing show in Las Vegas. As I "watched them burn," I was amazed that these guys didn't utter a *single word* throughout their performance! They interacted with the audience with exquisite timing and gestures. And I absolutely loved it!

Blue Man Group: 0% words, 100% message!

I think I may even return to enjoy their show again…

"Yes I *am…*"

"Yes I *am…*"

22. LEARNING STYLES

Different "Stokes" for Different Folks

In order to fuel our speaking fires, we must understand what fuels learning. There are three different types of learners. According to Richard Bandler's research into neuro-linguistic programming, there are three major channels through which people learn: visual, auditory, and kinesthetic. One key to successful captivation is to attempt to use all three of these in each presentation you give.

And sadly, this is rarely done. Almost all presentations are auditory. Some include the visual, as well, because of the use of PowerPoint. But there's so much more we could be doing. The kinesthetic learner is the least appreciated and serviced. This is the experiential learner, the "hands-on" person, who needs to be more directly involved.

Over the years I have compiled the following list of captivators that are guaranteed to ignite and maintain the "burning of learning." Consider the use of:

Props, toys, work tools, household gadgets, nature items, musical instruments, neon paper, worksheets, simulations, improvisations, skits, stories, songs, jokes, one-liners, games, cartoons, metaphors, movement, music, magic, lighting effects, sound effects, blue lights, memorized soliloquies, quotes, volunteers on stage, video clips, slides, set design, gifts to audience, candy, scents, "cool breeze" fans, rap, pantomime, role-plays, dance, meditation, quick-tally, "plants" in the audience, impressions, love-offerings, sharing the "mike," clothing, costumes, wigs, etc.

I invite you to use these, and I encourage you to brainstorm other ways to integrate these three crucial channels to "stoke up" your fires.

Chapter Seven

Warming Hearts Through Stories

Storytelling works because there is a child in all of us, waiting for a good story to be told.

—Bertram Minkin

You don't have to tell stories to be in the speaking business...only if you want to be successful.

—Unknown

The best leaders...almost without exception, and at every level, are masters of using stories and symbols.

—Tom Peters

Why is the sharing of personal stories so powerful? Why is personal sharing so needed, especially in corporate presentations? For one thing, it's an indispensable method for creating that intimate, captivating connection with your audience.

We make decisions with our heads.
We make commitments with our hearts.

—Lilly Walters

That's a large part of what speakers are, or should be, attempting to achieve. We want more from our audiences than mere intellectual decisions and affirmations; we want people committed to their resolves.

The heart of the matter is the heart.

And when we tell stories, we invite our listeners in from the sterile cold to enjoy the radiating warmth of a crackling fire along with a mug of hot, rich cocoa. Mmmm…

Self-Disclosure

When you share your personal stories, your fire will not only burn brighter, it will also burn longer. You will actually *live longer.* Honestly!

In his book, *The Transparent Self,* Dr. Sidney Jourard theorized that if we reveal ourselves to each other, we would live healthier, happier lives with less disease. Here are some excerpts from his book regarding the power of self-disclosure and the consequences of avoidance:

- **…We camouflage our true being before others to protect ourselves against criticism or rejection. This protection comes at a steep price.**

- **…When we succeed in hiding our being from others, we tend to lose touch with our real selves. This loss of self contributes to illness in its myriad forms.**

- **…In a poker game, no man discloses the contents of his hand to the other players. Instead, he tries to dissemble. If he holds four aces, he tries to get the** others to believe his hand is empty until it is time for the showdown. If he holds nothing, he pretends he has four aces; he tries to get something for nothing. In a society, which pits man against man, as in a poker game, people do keep a poker face; they wear a mask and let no one know what they are up to. In a society where man is for man, then the psychological iron curtain is dropped.

- …I became fascinated with self-disclosure after puzzling about the fact that patients who consulted me for therapy told me more about themselves than they had ever told another living person. Many of them said, "You are the first person I have ever been completely honest with." I wondered whether there was some connection between their reluctance to be known by spouse, family, and friends and their need to consult with a professional psychotherapist.

- …Every maladjusted person is a person who has not made himself known to another human being and in consequence does not know himself. Nor can he be himself. More than that, he struggles actively to avoid becoming known by another human being. He works at it ceaselessly, twenty-four hours daily, and it is work!

(A quick aside: Even though I consider *The Transparent Self* an excellent book, I found it ironic that the author reveals little about himself. He who so clearly saw the need for disclosure, did not himself disclose.)

Jourard's prediction has been confirmed by many scientific studies on health and longevity. George Vaillant studied over 250 Harvard alumni over the forty-plus years following their graduations. His study (aka: "The Great Study") was designed to discover the factors separating the healthy grads from the unhealthy ones. Incredibly, it turned out that the critical factor was neither diet, nor exercise, nor general fitness. The single most important key to health and well-being was *self-disclosure!*

Vaillant's study posed fundamental questions about how individuals cope differently with life's stresses. From his book on that study, *Adaptation to Life:*

Why do some of us cope so well with the portion life offers us, while others, who have had similar advantages (or disadvantages), cope badly or not at all? Are there ways we can effectively alter those patterns of behavior that make us unhappy, unhealthy, and unwise?

Some of the questions asked to those being studied were:

1. "Do you have trouble going for help and advice?"
2. "Can you talk about your oldest friends?"
3. "What made them friends?"
4. "What do people criticize you for or find irritating about you?"
5. "Have you ever seen a psychiatrist?"
6. "For how long?"
7. "What are your own satisfactions and dissatisfactions with yourself?"

Again, the amazing findings of this study argue that we can change destructive patterns of behavior and become happier and healthier by revealing **ourselves**. According to this study, we can conclude that self-disclosure through stories may be done, if for no other reason, for our *own* well-being.

But there is *another* reason — *another* benefit in sharing. We are, after all, speakers. We have a goal to **connect** with our audience. It is my theory that the avoidance and self-protection upon which Jourard comments is not only hard, misdirected, and fatiguing "work" — it is also extremely counter-productive toward our goal.

When a speaker refuses to open his *own* heart, there is *little* chance a listener will choose to open *theirs*.

In contrast, when a speaker self-discloses, particularly in areas most people vigilantly protect, it allows the listener to breathe relief. All of a sudden the energy level in the room signals to them it is *safe to relax — safe to be real*. Perhaps *this* is one of the most significant benefits of sharing personally. The audience may not realize it, but they are *relaxing* their hard-working, ever-vigilant, protective shells.

When an audience member relaxes their *ego protection defense system*, several **magical phenomena** occur:

- They feel intensely connected to the speaker. They may not even know why.
- Now that the room is "safe," the participant allows the challenges of the message to freely flow.
- Each listener is now ripe for self-discoveries – their own "aha's."
- Every audience member is now "pulling for you" to succeed.

When this happens, success is *guaranteed*.

When I previously used the term "magical phenomena," I was not exaggerating!

And yet, *very* few speakers choose to self-disclose! I have spent a *lifetime* at speaking events. I have listened to *thousands* of speeches on tapes. I know speakers all over the world. I *regularly* attend speaker's conventions.

And I can count the speakers who — in my opinion — truly, sincerely, openly share from their lives...**on two hands!**

TWO HANDS!

... I've heard all the "reasons."
... I've heard all the "philosophies."
... I've heard all the "explanations."
... I've heard all the "insights."

"The platform is not the place to discuss such issues."
Baloney!
"Some in the audience may not be ready for such talk."
Baloney!
"You're risking your credibility."
Baloney!
"If you share a weakness, it will be used against you later."
Baloney!

The sad truth is that many of the speakers who advise against self-disclosure use that *same* platform for *bragging*. And bragging has the exact *opposite* effect.

This only *stiffens* the defenses of the audience. These ego-signals "trip alarms," and the audience is now on *heightened alert* to prove they are *just fine*, but the *speaker* is not so perfect.

Bragging is platform suicide. Period!

And yet, if I were asked how many speakers I've heard *bragging*, there wouldn't be enough fingers to count them in an audience of *two thousand!*

The reason most speakers choose to brag rather than self-disclose is obvious. As we speakers glance into a sea of eyes, our insecurity may perceive these eyes as critical, judgmental, bored or hostile. This bristles our own defenses. Thus, we're now reluctant to bare our souls.

Combine this strong reluctance with the fact that audiences desire a more intimate, personal connection, and the boastful "expert" approach is nothing but a recipe for disaster. The self-disclosing, relatable approach is a recipe for a delicious meal, full of nutrition for the audience *and* the speaker!

Humility. Honesty. Authenticity. The best health insurance policy money *can't* buy and the recipe for your success. So the next time we stand before an audience and again behold that "sea of eyes," let's, instead, remember that those eyes are…

    … straining to witness a *warm* encounter.
    … looking for ways to *relate* to the speaker.
    … wanting to see a *human being* before them — a person with some *failings,*

as well as some *accomplishments*.

… wanting to see someone who is willing to *risk* being open and vulnerable.

Get the "drift"?

This *powerful* dynamic is achieved by offering *your* stories.

Sharing a personal story will impact your speech in a way that nothing else will, and remember…

… *it's healthy!*

Fourteen Storytelling Tips

*I*n my experience over the years, I've gathered several valuable pointers that I've found to be powerfully effective. I offer you these "Matchstick Tips" that are guaranteed to "fire up" your heartwarming stories:

Be Original

First, one of the powers of sharing *personal* stories is that it's guaranteed to be an *original* story, not a story anyone else has told. General, impersonal, overly retold stories just don't make the cut. (Please! No more "throwing starfish back into the ocean.") Be the original you were meant to be!

Don't Be The Hero

It's not about packaging but rather unwrapping.

—Jan Darcy

I once coached a president of a Fortune 500 company on a speech he was to deliver to his management staff of 200. The topic was "Favoritism," and John felt strongly about this injustice. He had his points organized, his statistics ready, and even a captivating introduction. I praised him for this and told him only one thing was still needed — personal sharing. This sparked a ten-minute discussion that included the following remarks:

"John, tell me of a time when you showed favoritism, and later realized it."

"I can't think of such an occasion."

"OK, think of a time when you were shown preferential treatment, and it made you feel uneasy."

"No luck there — I can't remember that ever happening to me."

"John, surely there has been one occasion in your life where favoritism was present."

"Well, there was one — when I was a child, only eight or nine. I had an uncle that called all of his nieces and nephews by their first names — except me. He called me — 'Reject.'"

Bingo! We had the story — certainly not of the "packaging" variety, but rather of the "unwrapping." John captivated the entire room as he shared what he felt when he was called "Reject." The speech was a crowning success, as this executive connected with his staff like never before!

Search Your Past

Occasionally, people come up after my speeches and say, "James, where did you get all those stories? Things like that *never* happened to me."

"Oh, yes they did. You've just *forgotten* them — some of them intentionally — because they were humbling or humiliating. Our defense mechanisms try to make us forget."

In fact, the stories we probably need the most are the ones most forgotten. The stories are there for all of you. You just have to dig for them. Begin your search here:

Ask your parents and family members...
- What about me upset you the most?
- What surprised you the most?
- What touched your heart the most?
- What about me concerned you the most?
- What did my teachers tell you about me?

Ask friends...
- How did I disappoint you the most? Let you down?
- When was I not there for you when you needed me?

Ask yourself...
- What was the funniest thing that ever happened to me?
- What was the apology I needed to give?
- How did my friend set me straight?
- What was my biggest "Aha"?
- What was my most embarrassing work experience?
- When was I given a second chance?
- What was the practical joke that was played on me?
- When did I really lose my cool?

And there are many more questions. Dig deeply. These are the ingredients of wonderful, heartwarming, connecting stories.

Search your past.

IV Affirm Your Ability

Affirm your storytelling ability! Many people don't do a good job of telling stories, only because they've convinced themselves they cannot. Never, never again utter statements like:

"I'm the worst storyteller."

"I always leave out the best part."

"No, you tell it. I can't."

The people who say these things are programming themselves to continue thinking this way.

Begin today, telling yourself:

"My life is brimming with captivating stories!"
"I'm excited to share with others what happened to me!"
"I tell stories well!"

Tell yourself these positive affirmations, and then enjoy the new storyteller you've become!

V Never Introduce Your Story

This is just professionalism. There's no need to preface your sharing with "This reminds me of a joke" or "This reminds me of a story." Just *tell* the story. It needs no "lead in" other than its proper place in your speech.

VI Inventory Your Stories

Keep a careful record of what you said, when you said it, to whom you said it, where you said it, what the occasion was, and what the point was. I keep meticulous records of my stories. Let's say you are speaking at The Center for Child Development. Assume you have spoken to them before. You know the message you want to deliver and you are trying to find an appropriate personal story to share. You find the perfect story, but, uh-oh, after checking, you discover that you'd given the same story to them eight months before — at a different location. It would have been a real mistake to use it again with the *same* crowd in that venue!

Remember, your stories are intended to connect and captivate. A story retold to the same group will accomplish neither. So, you might sometimes keep the same basic keynote speech. Just be sure to have *new* stories.

 **Prepare Two Versions**

Design and practice a *long* and *short* version of your major stories. Imagine it's near the end of your speech, and you want to close with one of your signature stories. You glance at your watch and notice you've only four minutes left. You need one minute after your story to close out the presentation. This allows you only three minutes. With two versions of your story — a six-minute and a three-minute — you have no need to panic! You now give the abbreviated version, and you still step off the riser a little *before* the scheduled time.

 **Use Your License**

"May I see your poetic license, please?"

You do have a poetic license, so feel free to use it.

"I am a creative artist," says Barry Mann, **"and that makes me different from a reporter. Reporters tell facts; storytellers tell truths."**

Well, yes… But let's make sure we have a very strong allegiance to the facts. Obviously, if you're flat out lying, your license is revoked. Each speaker must decide for himself or herself when stretching the truth becomes fibbing. In one book, what was considered "allowable stretching for dramatic purposes" did cross the line, in my opinion, into prevarication. This book's fundamental question seemed to be —

"Wouldn't it be more dramatic if instead…?"

For example, what actually happened was that you got locked out of your room, but wouldn't it be *more dramatic* if, instead, you got stuck in the elevator? If *fifty* people were waiting for you to speak, wouldn't it be *more dramatic* if it were *two hundred*? And maybe it shouldn't be *two hundred employees*, but instead *five hundred CEOs*?

I can only speak for myself, but I find that to be disingenuous and inauthentic. I'll stretch the truth a little myself, and maybe some others might find that too far off base. This is one area in which we must all decide for ourselves, and then strive hard not to critically judge others who choose differently.

IX   Revisit and Retell

Don't explain. *Revisit* and *retell*. Use the remembered dialogue and let us hear the conversation.

Version #1
Saying good-bye in the dormitory was more difficult than I had imagined. Now a college freshman, Alexandra would not be home for dinner each night. I thanked her for being such an awesome daughter, and she reciprocated. As I walked away, she reminded me to remember her, and her allowance!

Version #2
Saying good-bye in the dormitory was more difficult than I had imagined. Now a college freshman, Alexandra would not be home for dinner each night. I hugged her and said, "Thanks, Sweetie, for being such an awesome daughter — and friend."

While pulling back from my hug, she looked into my sad, but proud, eyes, and softly whispered, "Thanks, Dad, for always believing in me."

As I slowly walked away, tears began welling up as my mind tried to remember where the years had gone.

"Dad!"

Her voice shook me from my memories as her voice resonated down the hallway corridor.

"Dad! Don't forget me, and *especially* don't forget to send my allowance!"

…We both laughed, even through our tears.

Explained or retold… you decide.

 # Intersperse Humor

Build your stories with serious drama, interspersed with humor. Bring them from *tears* to *laughter*. (Can you spot where I used this technique in the above story?)

I have a story that almost always evokes tears. It involves a handwritten note of apology that my daughter, Alexandra, wrote to me years ago. As I'm reading the note, I can see people in the audience starting to get emotional. I read the final words: *"Love and kisses and apologies, Alex Lloyd."*

I turn and let them all see the note when I say, *"Alex Lloyd,"* and then I pause, and the audience looks up, many with tears in their eyes. So, I give them a few moments to let the heartwarming, tear-evoking story sink in. I then sprinkle in some humor…

"By the way, why do our children always include their *last* names when they write to us? 'Alex *LLOYD*.' As if I didn't know which 'Alex' it was!" Now, everybody is chuckling. And the humor doesn't have to be that funny to get them laughing because they need laughter at that moment. And it's the perfect time for them to wipe their tears as well. They've had a heart-warming moment, and now things can start fresh.

Dear Dad, I'm sorry that I wouldn't tell you when you asked me I was embarrased, I really hope you can forgive me. I'm also sorry that didn't appolgized sooner.

Love and Kisses, and appoligies,
X X X X O O O O ᴗ ᴗ ᴗ ᴗ ᴧ ᴧ ᴗ

Alex Floyd

Always Use Names

When telling a story, use names. If you can't remember a name, make one up. If you don't want to use someone's real name, make up another. This is the least of our poetic license liberties. When you do pick a name, be sure to *keep that name in that story*. You don't want someone coming up one day and telling you, "I was glad to hear 'The Sarah Story' again, James; but this time you used the name 'Josephine' instead of 'Sarah'!"

You've then lost credibility.

(Author's note: I make an exception to this rule when there is a negative implication. In such cases I refrain from names altogether.)

XII Never Brag

Don't tell stories in which you're the hero who saves the day. Leave that for Mighty Mouse. All you'll get for it from the audience is, "So what. Who cares?"

There once was a speaker who began her speech this way:

"When I was a junior in high school, I was ranked *fifth* in the nation in speaking. In my senior year, I was ranked *second*."

You can probably imagine how the audience reacted to that. A scattering of polite applause. Zero connection. Zero captivation.

(Suggestion — Never apologize for your successes, but always allow your introducer to highlight them for you… "Handing Over the Matches" — Chapter Three.)

XIII Make a Point

Connect the story with a point. Make it relevant to your message. Resist telling a story simply because it's entertaining. The difference between a story told by an entertainer and that told by a high-impact speaker is that the speaker's story should *illuminate a truth that relates to the speech*. The speaker's story should *touch* and *change* hearts and minds, not just tickle funny bones.

XIV Trim the Fat

Trim off the excess. Continue to edit and refine. Too many people have the basis for a wonderful story, but they've neither really worked with it nor adequately rehearsed it. Write those rough drafts. Then record the story on tape and listen to it as if you're in the audience. A second draft. Another recording. Change that word. Make sure you pause here…change the tone there…and put in a frown…right here. Now video it. Evaluate it. Refine it again and again, until it's the story you want — the *one that expresses you!*

One tell-tale sign that a story hasn't been worked or refined is when a speaker says, "To make a long story short…"

I don't believe in many "cardinal sins" in speaking, but this may be one. It proves that you didn't care enough about your own story to effectively fashion it. More importantly, you didn't care enough about your audience as well.

There's a proverbial saying in professional speaking:

"If you ever have to say, 'To make a long story short,'
it's probably *already* too late."

I invite you to use these "matchstick tips."
Strike them, and set fire to your stories.

When we speak from our mind,
we change people's minds.
When we speak from our heart,
we change people's hearts.
But when we speak from our life,
we change people's lives.

—Naomi Rhode

So, share yourself with us, please.

Warm our hearts.

Burn for us.

Tell us a story.

Your story!

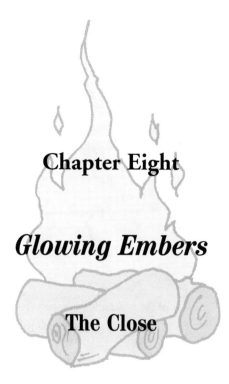

Chapter Eight

Glowing Embers

The Close

*T*oo often, speakers will spend hours and hours preparing the introduction and body of a speech and then give little thought to the close.

Salad…meat…spuds…but no memorable dessert.

There's an old speaker's adage that *tells* us:

> *1. Tell* **them what you're going to** *tell* **them.**
> *2. Tell* **them.**
> *3. Tell* **them what you told them.**

What a *predictable* and *boring* thing to do. We'll *never* captivate using this method. Our audience will tune us out pronto if all we're doing is summarizing what we've already said.

Other speakers simply rely on the message of the speech-proper to carry them through to their conclusion. They figure the right words will magically come to them, and they'll be able to basically *wing it* for the "winding down."

Huge mistake!

Winding down takes some winding up.

The close is a great opportunity to make *another* unique impact on the audience.

Use your close...
> ...as a call to action...
> > ... as a *striking* conclusion...
> > > ...to etch an indelible image...
> > > > ... to make a persuasive appeal...
> > > > > ...or to present a new thought to ponder.

Be creative with your close.

Make this lasting impression *memorable!*

Memorize it. If there are any parts of your speech that should be totally memorized, they are the *introduction* and the *close*. In the introduction, you're establishing connection and credibility. The close is for that final punch — not a wrap-up or a recap. Practice that punch. Think of it as that sweet uppercut that will finish the match. **Knock out!**

And when you close — ***close.*** Don't go into your landing only to pull out of it time and time again —
> "Oh, one more thing..."
> "Oh, I forgot to tell you..."
> "Oh, this is important..."

Not only would you be taking all the "punch" out of your "pitch," but it's irritating as well. Keep circling around, and members of the audience may begin exiting the aircraft.

I'm reminded of a workshop that I conducted in California. A successful female executive gave a presentation, and it was a captivating, passionate speech. However, what I remember most is when it came time for her to close, she just froze. She blankly stared at us for a few moments, then said:

"That's all I have to say…about that."

With that, she sat down.

And, to be honest, that's *all* I remember about her speech. I do remember that she was vibrant, entertaining, and thought provoking. But I cannot tell you *what* the speech was about, *what* facts were shared, or *what* points she made. All that's *burned* in my brain is that horrible close.

No preparation, no practice.

No punch, no power.

Her fire burned out…

"…and that's all I have to say about that."

—Forrest Gump

The Close After the Close

The presentation is not over until everyone in the room has left, and you are alone. You may not really be alone until you're in your car, back in your hotel room, or on a flight back home. But until you get to that place, your presentation is *still* happening. And you'd better believe that impressions are *still* being made!

Warning! Warning!

At this point, we are most vulnerable.

We're *spent*.

Our fuel reserves are *low*.

We're *drained* and *exhausted*.

Our flint pouches are *empty*.

Very few people realize the amount of energy expended in one hour of "on-fire" speaking. But we *must* remember: our speeches evoke emotions, passions, questions, and memories for our listeners.

—They've heard our stories and now they want to tell us theirs!
—The flint has been shared. Now, *they* are on fire.

They may want to share with us their own situations.

They may want advice.

(They may want to *offer* advice!)

And unless we are very careful at this point, we can undermine all that we've worked so hard to achieve.

To prevent this, I suggest that we always give our fullest attention to that "listener" who is ready to speak.

It requires *focus* to fully engage each and every one of them.

It requires *love* to find ways to honor them.

Mary Sigmann remembers hearing the powerful Maya Angelou speak one evening. She remembers even more pointedly what Maya shared with her afterwards:

> "Thank you for being such a responsive listener. I really appreciate your being in the audience." Now *that* is a lasting impression!

There will be times when audience members may request a copy of a poem you've used, or an extra handout. If you take their business cards and promise to get those things to them — *follow through!* Otherwise, the most lasting impression they'll have of you is that you didn't send them that which you promised.

I usually have my personal audio-recorder on during and after a speech. I record the speech for obvious reasons — to edit, polish, perhaps even to sell — but I leave it on so that when people come up to speak with me afterwards, I'll have *that* taped as well. Later, I can listen to it and evaluate my responses.

Was I interactive?

Was I fully attentive?

Sometimes, people will approach me and ask if I can speak for their company or group. When they do, I'll have all their information without having to get out my notebook and write down details about their situations, their needs, or conference dates. (When I later refer to those comments or details, they are usually pleasantly surprised.)

As our embers are in their final glow, the fire of our message has hopefully been passed on successfully to others. By now, I'm sure you're expecting me to stop circling and land. So please turn the page for the final chapter.

And I promise you more than a recap.

Chapter Nine

The Three Burning Questions

I know that I'm taking a considerable risk…by including this chapter on a topic that I've not seen in any other book on speaking. I'm taking a risk…in telling you that I believe it to be the most important chapter in this book. I'm taking a risk…by playing my song before you, attempting in written form, a tune that has worked well for me through the lyricism of speech. I hope that you won't find it too discordant or unavailing. But, then, taking risks *is* a crucial part of what this chapter is all about…

that…

and love…

and making a difference.

I was given a helpful book during the darkest days of my life. My mother was dying of cancer. I had been having great difficulty coping. The book was *The Power of Purpose*, by Richard Leider. In both this book and other writings I discovered research about dying that profoundly altered my life.

According to Leider, there are three universal questions that people ask themselves when they are close to death:

1. "Did I give and receive love?"

2. "Did I play my music?"

3. "Did I make a difference?"

Again, it is not the rare individual who asks themselves these burning questions; we as a species seem inherently wired to do so. It is this "wiring" that ensures a potent connection with every audience when these questions are properly approached and applied in our presentations.

These can be very chilling, even heart-breaking, questions, especially when people wait until they are on their deathbeds to ask them.

Most of us go to our graves with our music still inside us.

—Oliver Wendell Holmes

These searing questions need not be asked at the eleventh hour. We are not anxious students who have cleared our desks in expectation of this final exam.

I think back to my college experience. I wasn't the finest student or the best prepared. I dreaded those closed-book exams, but once in a while, a generous professor would announce an "open-book" final. So that we could best direct our study, he would give us *all* of the test questions a few days beforehand. What a break! How lucky!

I now had the questions and knew what to research. I felt so confident! What more could I have asked for? *No excuses for not doing well!*

Now that we have received these burning questions, what excuses do we have? Each of us now has been given **THE ULTIMATE** open-book exam! We have the challenge and the opportunity to begin preparing now — today — and every day from now on!

"These are certainly existential questions," you're probably saying. "But how does taking this 'test' now develop my skills as a speaker?"

Well, it's my belief that anything that affects a significant change in you as a person will affect changes in those around you. You will present yourself differently. You will work differently. And your friends and loved ones will both see and react to you differently…and so will your audiences.

These three questions also serve as wonderful "barometers."

At the end of each speech I deliver, I ask myself…

- **"Have I loved my audience?"**

- **"Have I played my music and given the participants opportunities to play their music as well?"**

- **"Have I not only made a difference to them, but have I additionally shown them that they make a difference?"**

So that you can enjoy the magical power of these three questions in your presentations, let's further explore each one.

1. Did I give and receive love?

The two things people need most are love and appreciation. These two needs do not magically change on Monday morning when they go to work.

*T*hese are not the words of a minister or a transcendentalist. This is a quotation from Herb Kelleher, the founder of Southwest Airlines. The word "appreciation" is often used in corporate America. The word "love"…*rarely*.

> **I am mystified by the fact that the business world is apparently proud to be seen as hard and uncaring and detached from human values…the word "love" was as threatening in business as talking about a loss on the balance sheet. Perhaps that is why using words like "love" and "care" is so difficult in today's extraordinarily macho business world. No one seems to know how to put the concept into practice… I think all business practices would improve immeasurably if they were guided by "feminine" principles – qualities like love and care and intuition.**
>
> **—Anita Roddick, founder of The Body Shop**

Anita is a successful businesswoman who is certainly concerned with profits and losses. But she also understands that success in business can be improved with love and care. So can our speeches!

In his book, *How to Win Friends and Influence People*, author Dale Carnegie writes about Howard Thurston, the "Dean of Magicians":

> **He knew many magicians would look at the audience and say to themselves, "Well, there is a bunch of suckers out there, a bunch of hicks; I'll fool them all right."**
> **But Thurston's method was totally different. Every time he went on stage, he said to himself, "I am grateful because these people have come to see me. They make it**

possible for me to make my living in a very agreeable way. I'm going to give them the very best I possibly can."

He declared he never stepped in front of the footlights without first saying to himself over and over, "I love my audience. I love my audience."

More than *60 million* people — not "suckers," not "hicks" — paid to see him perform.

It is not hard to see why.

Herb, Anita, and Howard did not shrink from using the word *"love"*…

…neither should we.

They succeeded by *loving*

...as can we.

How can we, as speakers, love our audiences?

Consider the following:

> **All audiences have certain things in common. For one thing, they all want you to talk about them, not about you. They want to feel that you have their interests at heart. So it's helpful if you actually do have their interests at heart.**
>
> **...As hard as it can be to believe, your speaking engagement is not primarily about you. It's about them.**
>
> **—*Taking Center Stage*, by Gottesman and Mauro**

Sad to say, many speakers *never* grasp this truth. But until you do, it's going to be hard to love your audience. There are many aspects within the concept of love that can also be grasped and delivered tangibly: acknowledgment, appreciation, recognition, and respect, to name a few. People who sense these affirmations from you will be eager to sit in those front rows, eager to grasp your "love." Love's flames burn brightest, and those who are warmed by the light will, indeed, be captivated!

> **A successful man is one who can build a firm foundation with the bricks that others throw at him.**
>
> **—David Brinkley**

One challenging, yet rewarding, way to love an audience is to *handle negative people with poise and respect.* I was once in New York City conducting a half-day training for a group of salespeople with whom I'd never spoken before. Just to begin connecting with the group, I started out complimenting them on the great city they had:

"My name is *Ja-ames Lloy-oyd*, and it's a total *dee-ligh-ight* to be here with you this morning in the *Bi-ig* Apple…"

…and that was as far as I got with my Southern accent before someone raised his hand. A bit surprised by the interruption so soon, I still acknowledged him, "Yes?"

And this gentleman I'd never met before began speaking in a Southern drawl.

"*Excu-use* me, but where are *y'all* from?"

It was obvious to me that this man was making fun of my accent, and since it happened right at the beginning of my speech, his rudeness threw me off a bit. But I kept my cool, gave the audience a smile and replied, "'Y'all'? Oh, well 'y'all' is from Atlanta, Georgia, and I've lived most of my life in the Southeast. Four years ago, I moved out to Los Angeles, where I now live."

I then got back to my introduction. Or tried to.

"So it's a pleasure for me to be to here today, and I want you to know…"

And that same man raised his hand again.

"Yes?"

"You say you're from Atlanta? You're not another John Rocker are you?"

(For those of you who are unaware of who John Rocker is, God has blessed you. You've been spared. For those who are aware, I hope you can appreciate the awkwardness I felt. John Rocker, at the time, was a baseball pitcher for the Atlanta Braves. During a road trip to New York, a writer from *Sports Illustrated* interviewed him about his experiences in New York City. In one paragraph, Rocker was able to malign every minority: Blacks, gays, Hispanics, single mothers, Yankees… He caused a lot of furor and from then on needed lots of security whenever he went to New York. He was considered the consummate "redneck.")

After taking a moment to compose myself, I explained to this man and to the audience, "I want you to know, I'm no John Rocker. Rocker is an embarrassment to the vast majority of people who live in the South, and in many ways set us back in terms of the reputation we want to have around the country and around the world. I assure you, I'm no John Rocker."

I then went back to my introductory remarks. One more attempt:

"I just got into New York last night and found I couldn't sleep. I simply *had* to go to Times Square, just to see what was going on. After all, this is the city that never sleeps. When I got down there, I was delighted to see 'Ray's Pizza'!" (For those who don't know, Ray's Pizza is the *finest* pizza in the world.) I continued:

"I'm something of a connoisseur of pizza, having sampled it from all over this country and from most pizza-cooking countries throughout the world; and I believe I've established enough credibility to say that Ray's may well be number one! Ray's is the pizza sent to presidential inaugurations — it's the pizza shipped all over the world. And I was ecstatic to eat a couple of slices of Ray's Pizza at one o' clock in the morning…"

Well, that man's hand shot up one more time. And I was thinking, "What is it with him? What now? Oh no, here come the fat jokes."

"Yes, sir," I responded.

"So you ate Ray's Pizza last night?" he asked. "At the one in Times Square?"

"Yes, I did."

Then he chuckled and added, "That's not the *real* Ray's Pizza. The *real* Ray's is still in Greenwich Village on…" (and he gave the address). "That one you ate at last night in Times Square? That's a shop they just put in there for the *dumb tourists!*" And he sat back with a smile.

I realized then that I'd been speaking for less than a minute, and in that time I'd had my **accent mocked**, been called a **redneck bigot**, and now a **dumb tourist!** I have to say that it was the closest I'd ever come to just shutting up the books, stopping the speech, and just giving that man a real piece of my mind (*or something else*). He deserved it so much, and I was so indignant! But that's when those burning questions entered my mind:

> **"Did I give and receive love?"**

> **"Have I loved the audience?"**

So…I smiled. I'll tell you, it wasn't easy. But I smiled…and loved:

"Thank you for letting me know where the *real* Ray's is located. I've got just enough time today after the training is over to have the taxi-driver stop at that address. I'm writing it down right now; and I'll have the real Ray's Pizza, *thanks to you*."

I'm not inferring that this was easy for me. It was actually *quite difficult…*

…and effective.

Never attack a member of the audience. **"Hating people,"** comments Harry Emerson Fosdick, **"is like burning down your house to get rid of a rat."**

Had I attacked this offensive man, I would have burned down the house, ruining the connection I was establishing with the rest of the audience. An insightful person once observed that there are two kinds of people: those who have ulcers and those who are carriers. If I'd gotten in his face, it would have made him a more potent carrier.

I went back to my presentation, and that man was respectful for the next three hours. At the end of our time together, around noon, he came up to me and apologized for his earlier comments. To this day, I don't know why he changed his attitude. Perhaps some of his colleagues approached him during a break and explained that he was way off base. Or perhaps it was the respect and appreciation I showed him that won him over. Either way, I had loved my audience.

By the way, Ray's slogan is "Nobody Leaves Hungry" and this certainly applied to me, as I enjoyed that *ENTIRE* pizza in a New York cab!

So, loving our audiences is critical. And it's certainly not easy to do when we have critical audience members. But we *can* respect them and *thank* them. We can usually *find something positive* in their remarks.

I gained invaluable experience with disrespectful people when I was a minister working in London. I'd go regularly to Speaker's Corner in Hyde Park. It was an amazing venue. Dozens of speakers would be there every weekend, usually standing on a box or crate, speaking without microphones. The louder the voice, the greater the crowd. Literally hundreds, sometimes thousands, of people would be wandering from speaker to speaker, looking for the one who was the most captivating. And, oh, the hecklers! It was my theory that this was the international training ground for hecklers. These outspoken disrupters were pros. Mostly a British crowd, as I remember, and I was an irresistible target for them, a heckler's dream: American, religious, and a Southern accent to boot! I presented an unparalleled multiplicity of targets!

**"Hey, Yank! Go back to your peanut farm...
and take your religion with you!"**

I learned to keep my cool and to love them. I'd talk to some people afterwards and they'd tell me what great practice it must be for handling hecklers. But I was looking at the deeper opportunity and would say, "Yeah, great practice for hecklers, but even greater practice for loving the unlovable."

I recall Martin Luther King, Jr.'s statement:

The ultimate measure of a man is not where he stands in moments of comfort, but where he stands at times of challenge and controversy.

How you react to those that taunt you reveals the real you. It's *easy* to be a glamorous, fantastic speaker in moments of comfort, when everything is set just perfectly, and the audience loves you. It's *easy* to be loving when security is standing by to escort out anyone who interrupts you. But the time may come when your speaking may invite challenge and controversy. Do you have the ability to respect and love your "hecklers"? How you handle *this* situation is the ultimate measure of your love for your audience.

It is my theory — mine because I've never heard anyone claiming this before —

There Are No Bad Audiences!

No bad audiences — there are only bad speakers, bad messages, inadequate research, poor connections, lack of appreciation and respect, lack of humility on the speaker's part — but *no* bad audiences!

One book I read regarding presentation skills suggested that a speaker classify every audience, prior to the engagement, as either an "A-audience" or a "B-audience." The A-audience would be eager and positive; the B-audience negative, and only there to vent frustration or be entertained. Again, this is done prior to going before them.

Self-righteously prejudging an audience! Obviously, this conflicts with my theory. I try hard to never prejudge, and I'm determined to believe that there are "no bad B-audiences." Now, I'll admit this is easier said than done. But the beauty of my theory is that if a speech doesn't go well, you're forced to look at what *you could have done better*. You cannot throw it on the audience because *you* don't *have* that option. And I can't tell you how many times I *so* wanted to blame it on the audience. But I refuse that cop out! In my opinion, when you classify an audience as a "B-audience," you're really only classifying *yourself* a "B-speaker"!

Recently, a high school football coach invited me to give a motivational speech to his team. They'd been on a losing streak, and he thought a rousing, motivating speech might help turn things around. I spent some time preparing, but there was one thing for which I couldn't prepare. I'd never spoken to an audience of high school boys, much less a losing high school football team. My speech was *awful*. I could not connect with them at all! I had six attempts at humor; one got smiles, and that was the best of all the responses to anything I said that night. My personal sharing didn't connect either. I just couldn't "rev 'em up."

When I left, a couple of parents asked me how it went. I confessed that I'd never bombed so thoroughly in my life. Oh, how I wanted to blame it on the team and say:

"What in the world is it with high school teenagers today?"

"No wonder they can't win a game; they're lifeless and boring!"

But there are **no** *bad audiences*. And after some reflection, I thought that if I'd started things out with some magic tricks, had a little fun with that first, and got them involved, it probably would have broken the ice, established some rapport, and my "Knute Rockne" might have been more successful. (By the way, they lost the next game and I haven't been invited back since.)

A few years ago I took advantage of a grand opportunity. While enjoying Amsterdam for a few days, I visited the home of Anne Frank. At such a young age, she stunned the world with her positive attitude. **"People,"** wrote Anne Frank in her diary, **"are basically good."** I remember staring at that journal entry, amazed that anyone could view mankind that graciously during the Holocaust! Whenever I think of her statement, I remain overwhelmed and humbled. If Anne could remain so compassionate in her deplorable situation, I can do the same with my audiences…

While working for AchieveGlobal, I did a lot of training for a phone company call center in Dallas. I was scheduled for a Monday/Tuesday class of new hires. This group of twenty was a little larger than I would normally teach. Since all the other classes had gone well, I was excited about it. But on the Friday before the Monday-start, I got a call from the director of training. He told me the training had been called off for Monday and Tuesday, so I was not to come.

Now, that had me greatly concerned because, as an independent consultant, I only got paid for training days. Even though the official policy allowed me 50% of my daily rate when a class was canceled so close to the start date, I needed 100%.

More than that, however, I was curious how a training class could be canceled that abruptly.

"What happened? Why is it being canceled?"

"I can't tell you. But we've decided to give you your full rate anyway."

Of course, I was grateful for that, but still curious. I said, "I'd still like to know why you canceled it."

After some cajoling, he finally confessed, "James, this is a group of new hires that we never should have hired." (They'd already been with the company for about three weeks, evidently, and I was to have trained them in customer service.)

"…Something happened today with that group that has never happened before with this company," he elaborated. "And it was very embarrassing."

"What in the world happened?"

"I was teaching them today, and they were being very unruly and disrespectful; and finally, I'd had enough. I said to them, 'You know what? You're all a bunch of kids who have no respect for anybody.' And then I started swearing."

"Oh, no," was all I could say.

"Yeah, I know you're going to say I should never have done that, but I had had *enough* from them. They *never* should have been hired! They're all minorities, all very young. For most of them, it's the first job they've ever had. James, I let them out today for the two o'clock break — they didn't come back!"

"You mean that they came back *late?*"

"No — I mean they *did not come back at all!* They just took off!"

I was astounded! "You didn't know where they were?"

"No. We eventually managed to round up most of them. But, by then, it was too late to continue. So, we just sent them home."

"Where were they?" I, of course, asked next.

"Well, a bunch of them were in the cafeteria. We found five of them down by the lake…" (This was, by the way, a beautiful complex with several fountains and even a gorgeous lake.)

"…And four of them went over to the movie theater next door. Frankly, we don't know *what* we're going to do now."

"So, you don't even know if they're going to come on Monday?"

"Nope."

"Are they fired?"

"Can't fire them because it's a union situation, and they haven't had the warnings and everything else. Right now, *we're stuck*."

"You know, I'd love to still come and talk to this group."

"No, no. You don't want to come, James. I don't know if they're going to be here; but even if they are, there's no need for you to come."

"No, I *want* to come," I insisted. "I want to see how well I can work with a group like this."

I came in on Sunday night and was in class early on Monday. The director couldn't believe I actually was there. He informed me that the only rule he had for this training was that I was *not* to let them out for breaks. I told him I couldn't keep people for two days without giving them breaks. After some consideration, he bargained —

"All right, I'll tell you what. You let them out for breaks, and if they take off, *you* chase them down!"

I nervously agreed, "That's a fair deal."

The director hadn't misled me in one area. Everyone was awfully young. I guess the average age was eighteen or nineteen. The thought of not giving them breaks was unimaginable. I wouldn't do that to any mature group, let alone these trainees who were young and energized.

Soon, they were all in and seated. The first thing I always do with students, after warmly welcoming them, is to give them a few respectful ground rules. I told them that everyone has permission to ask questions and make mistakes because that's part of the learning process. It's also okay to take breaks. And when I discussed breaks, I explained this the same way I'd done in every class I had ever taught — whether it was for CEOs, managers, or new hires. I told them:

"Our group will take regular breaks throughout the day. However, if you feel you need a break when the class doesn't, feel free to take one at *any* time. Please do not ask me for permission to take a break. You don't have to tell me where you're going or when you're coming back. I trust that if you're leaving the room, it's for a good reason. You may come back from a group break and realize that you forgot to do something. Don't apologize for that. Just extend the break. That's fine.

We may have some cigarette smokers in the room. I don't smoke, but I have friends who do, and they'll tell me that sometimes they want a cigarette so badly that they have a hard time concentrating. If that's the situation, please excuse yourself and enjoy your smoke.

All I ask is that you try to spend as much time in here as you can, so that you will not miss too much of this potentially life-changing program."

When I'd finished, the first hand of the day went up in the back of the room. "Hey, Teach."

"Yes, sir," I said. (It was the first time I'd ever been called "Teach.")

"You're saying we can leave for break *any time we want?*"

"That's exactly right."

"Haven't you heard anything about this group?"

"Yes, I've heard a *whole lot* about this group, to be honest with you."

"Then why are you giving us permission to leave any time we want?"

I paused for a moment, then began explaining, while making deliberate eye contact with those around the room.

"Because...I decided a *long* time ago...that if I were training, or if I were speaking, I would treat every person in the room the way *I* would want to be treated if *I* were sitting in the audience."

While nodding, the participant added, "That's pretty cool, Man."

The two-day training turned out to be one of the finest two days of training I've ever experienced. Sure, there were more than a few bumps along the road. They were a fairly rambunctious group. But not one person in that class ever came back late from a break! The learning that took place, the awareness, the "aha's," the mutual respect — all were wonderful!

And I had a few "aha's" of my own. I learned the importance of being patient and caring and respectful, and I learned that there is no such thing as a bad audience. I left Dallas with a new resolve. I would, from that day forward, initiate love and respect with my future audiences.

With That Moon Language

Admit something:
Everyone you see,
You say to them,
"Love me."
Of course, you do not say this out loud;
Otherwise, someone would call the cops.
Still though, think about this,
This great pull in us to connect.
Why not become the one
Who lives with a full moon in each eye
That is always saying,
With that sweet moon language,
What every other eye in this world
Is dying to hear.

—Hafiz

Connect "with that sweet moon language" of respect, appreciation, and love. Then, with a "full moon in each eye," you can fill those empty front row seats with an eager "A-audience" *dying to hear* your words.

A seasoned trainer once shared with me, "There are two captivating radio stations that transmit appreciation, love, and respect to an audience."

"Two radio stations?" I asked puzzled.

"You heard right. There's both an AM and FM station…"

…That was ten years ago.

Tuning in to these stations has elevated my ability to love.

I now share their "power" with you…

W I I — F M

The vast majority of speeches and presentations that I have heard fail to address a most important factor — "**W**hat's **I**n **I**t **F**or **M**e?" That's what audience members are asking before the presentation even starts.

> "Is this worth my time?"
> "Why am I here?"
> "Will this be of use to me?"
> "WII-FM?"

I've witnessed finance presentations with slides that most people in the audience found boring and difficult to understand because these slides lacked relevance. So, I've coached finance executives, "If you can just show the participants a slide and explain, 'This profit line means, as long it stays in the positive, *you keep your budget*. As soon as it goes under and goes to red, that's when we start *cutting back budgets*.' Now executives and other managers in the audience will look differently at those slides and charts because they can see how it applies to them — *what's in it for them.*"

Now there's relevance...

WII-FM has been tuned in...and the audience is listening.

I now "tune in" to this station every time I address an audience. I've tried to do likewise in this book. In the Introduction I showed you how you can personally benefit from improving your presentation skills. Remember the individual who received a promotion, and my friend who was given more money than he'd even asked for? This is the "What's in it for me?" for this book. I hoped to inspire you, to keep you interested and entertained. And if you're reading this, perhaps it's worked.

The second radio station is equally as important, yet tuned in even less often!

MMFG — AM

Before my speech, I envision every audience member actually raising a hand and saying, "Excuse me, but I have a request. At some point during your presentation, could you **M**ake **M**e **F**eel **G**ood **A**bout **M**yself?"

Then, I picture myself complimenting each of them. I ponder:

What have they accomplished?

What awards have they won?

What hardships have they endured?

What obstacles have they overcome?

How have they contributed to their company's success?

"Tune in" to these questions, and watch what happens!

A company for which I once worked had purchased another company in Chicago. It was a rough acquisition. Financially, it was fine. But on the personal side, it left much to be desired. I felt like we had come in as a "bully" company and used this bulldozing philosophy: "We don't care what you used to do and who you used to be. Now, you're us, and it's time you start doing things our way." I went to speak to their sales force two months after the acquisition. Before the presentation, I'd asked for some of the success stories that this company had prior to merging with us, so that I could use these stories in my speech. One of our company's vice presidents told me:

"Oh, you don't have to bring up anything about their past. That's gone now. They're with us now, and they'll do as we would have them do."

He was a VP. He had authority over me. But I do have a healthy dose of productive defiance. I realized that what this group of people needed right now, more than anything else, was to feel good about themselves. I needed to tune them in to **MMFG-AM**. I had to let them know that they were important to us — that we needed them.

Before I addressed them, I noticed a plaque on the wall. It had been presented to this company for a superb radio advertisement. So, I copied all the facts and figures. Then I saw another award that they'd received from the City of Chicago for their stellar service. I wrote that down too.

I started my presentation, "What a *thrill* it is to be merging with such a top quality, blue-chip company!"

When I said that, eyes that were turned down began to look up at me.

"Congratulations on your *Golden Mike Award!*"

People began to smile. Next, I recognized their award from the city of Chicago, adding that I didn't remember our company ever getting an award like that from our city.

"This is absolutely tremendous! And let me tell you, we have a *lot* to learn from you and your successes."

I didn't expect anyone to speak up, but one woman, in tears, raised her hand.

"Thank you for those compliments! You'll never know how much we needed to hear those words right now."

After that, I could have flubbed the rest of the speech big time,

> could have stumbled over my words,
>
> forgotten what I wanted to say,
>
> dropped my notes on the floor…
>
> and *none* of it would have mattered.

Why? Because I'd truly connected with that audience through love. And that's magical. All I had to do was…

…tune in to those two radio stations, **WII-FM** and **MMFG-AM**…

…and the rest fell favorably into place.

…love covers over a multitude of sins.

—1 Peter 4:8
New International Version

If I have prophetic powers, and understand all mysteries and knowledge and if I have all faith, so as to remove mountains, but have not love, I am nothing.

—1 Corinthians 13:2
Revised Standard Version

2. Did I play my music?

You were born an original. Don't die a copy.

—John Mason

Whenever I present this "burning question," I'll ask, "What is the meaning of 'playing my music'?" This elicits responses such as…

"Did I live up to my potential?"

"Did I use my talents?"

"Did I go for it?"

"Did I take enough risks?"

Taking risks ensures originality. Taking risks also ensures fear. The following poem stirs me to take risks. It encourages me to play my own symphony in the performance hall of life.

Risk

To laugh is to risk appearing the fool.

To weep is to risk appearing sentimental.

To reach out for another is to risk exposing our
true self.

To place your ideas and dreams before the crowd
is to risk loss.

To love is to risk not being loved in return.

To live is to risk dying.

To hope is to risk despair.

To try at all is to risk failure.

But to risk we must!

Because the greatest hazard in life is to

    risk nothing—

The man and woman who risks nothing,

      has nothing,

          does nothing,

              is nothing.

                            —Unknown

When I was first hired by AchieveGlobal, they flew me to Las Vegas for a five-day certification program. The first three days were instructional. The last two were spent actually doing a couple of forty-minute presentations in front of the leader and the group. While preparing for my Thursday presentation on Wednesday night, instead of simply doing my assignment, I risked it. Wanting to impress everyone with my creativity, I went *way* out of bounds and came up with some wild exercises that I hoped would dazzle them all. The next day, during my presentation, I proudly unveiled my elaborate, intricate, complex exercise to the group! Knighthood would not be far away! And…

…It bombed!

I'll spare you the details (and spare myself the painful memories of dazed expressions, empty stares, and total silence)…

…It bombed!

Never in my life had I been so humiliated. Never had my ego been so blistered. My boss, Kelli Lynn, quickly called for a break. During that break, alone with Kelli Lynn, I did something I hadn't done in years… I cried…just sat there…and cried.

Turning to my manager, I began mumbling.

"I blew it. I was trying something new, and it bombed. You're probably regretting ever hiring me..."

She interrupted my confession by handing me a brightly colored paper. On it, written in bold neon letters were the words:

Keep Taking Risks!!!

(I still treasure this piece of paper.)

I continued to risk during my presentations...

     I once played the trumpet.

     I've tried new humor.

     I've used pyrotechnics. (Great balls of fire!)

     I involved the audience, even handed *them* the microphone.

     I attempted new magic feats.

     I brought one of my dogs on stage (darling Chi-Chi, the Chihuahua).

These are but a few of the ways I've "played my music."

And "playing your music" is sometimes risky!

Once I was invited to do a speech on "change." Just to create a different ambiance, I came dressed as a hippy (Jerry Garcia reincarnated). This was risky. Why? What if my costume overshadowed my message? What if people thought I was foolish?

But I love to risk it. It surges the adrenaline, and captivates the audience. This, from Debbie Ford's book, *The Dark Side of The Light Chasers*:

Our fear tells us not to take risks. It stops us from enjoying our richest treasures. Our fear keeps us living in the middle of the spectrum instead of embracing the full range.

Kelli Lynn encouraged me to keep taking risks, to "embrace my full range."

I love you for that, Kelli Lynn. Thank you so much for helping me play my music!

But it's not just finding ways to play *your* music. There's also magic in helping others to find and play *theirs*.

For example, there's Don and his "music." I met Don when I first moved to California. He was in a training class of mine. I noticed that he was always picking up the colored markers around the room and drawing pictures. And *wonderful* drawings they were. This man was truly talented! At the end of the first day, he came up and showed me what he'd drawn — a stunning illustration of my name. It was very well done — professionally done! He knew that I did magic, so he had cleverly drawn playing cards all over it, along with various magic symbols.

"Have you ever drawn professionally, Don?"

"No, I've just done things on the side for pleasure." (He later showed me his cubicle, where he had displayed various other drawings, including an extraordinary likeness of Michael Jordan.)

"Don, you could make a lot of money doing this," I told him, and asked what kind of equipment he had.

"I don't have anything, just those markers that you had in class."

Well, I shook his hand, left work during break, and went straight to Staples. There, I bought a nice drawing pad and a collection of fifty fine-point colored markers. I gave those items to him when I returned that afternoon, and encouraged him to continue drawing. In my mind, I was saying:

"Play your music, Don. Play your music."

And play it he did! He drew more pictures and more people saw them. When there came an opening in the training department for someone who could not only train, but do some advertising and marketing, Don was the obvious creative talent needed. He was hired and currently works in that position. He is loving it, and everyone is loving his "masterpieces."

When I decided to write this book, I thought of Don and asked him if he would be my illustrator. He was delighted to do so. What was amazing to me was that he didn't even want to be paid! (But I insisted.)

Keep playing your music, Don!

Start playing your music, speakers!

Play *your* music!

And in so doing, you'll encourage your audiences to play *theirs*.

Come To The Edge

"Come to the edge," he said.
They said, "We are afraid."
"Come to the edge," he said.
They came.
He pushed them...
...and they flew.

—Guillaume Apollinaire

3. Did I make a difference?

I once saw a bumper sticker that read:

"Make a living, not a difference."

Now, I know it was intended to be humorous, but I thought, how sadly true. It's just what so many people are doing.

I think it's so important that we search for the "worthwhileness" of our presentations — and don't present until we find it. Beforehand, if I cannot think of the statement in my speech that will make the difference, that speech is not yet ready to give.

After every speech, I ask myself, *"Did I make a difference?"*

After every day, I ask myself, *"Did I make a difference?"*

There are days when I answer…"No."

I then think of situations where I could have handled things better. Could I have been more creative and innovative — perhaps more compassionate or patient? What else could I have done to make a difference?

There's a definite connection between worthwhileness and passion. You can see one brick mason at work and ask what he's doing.

"I'm building a *wall*," he replies.

You see another brick mason and ask the same question.

"I'm building a *home*," he answers.

Each is performing the same task, but they have different perspectives, different philosophies. Perhaps, too, a different quality of work. One probably finds it much easier to "call in sick." After all, he only has bricks waiting for him, while the other has a family depending on him.

In our speeches, are we building *walls* or *homes?*

If we've shown love,

      if we've played our music,

           then we've made a difference.

After a speech, when I ask myself if I've made a difference, one of the criteria I consider is whether or not I've empowered my listeners.

Have I shown them that they are important?

Have I proven that each of them makes a unique difference?

Following are some techniques I've used to achieve this:

- Through the Internet, I thoroughly research the company I'm going to address. I try to find out exactly what they do, how they contribute to the economy and society, what awards they've won, which employees have received awards, and why. I gather all the "wood" I can.

- I always arrive early for a speech. If the speech is at seven o'clock, I'm there at least by six. I greet the audience members. I converse with them and take notes. I ask what they do, why they do it. I get them to talk about themselves and their work. I'll write down some of their statements and opinions and ask if I might use their words in my speech and credit them for it in front of their peers. (I've never been refused this honoring process.)

- If my speech is on the second day of a two-day affair, I'll try to be there the first day just to meet people. Often, I won't even tell them that I'll be the one speaking the next night. If it's an affair that offers a dinner the night before I speak, I try to attend that dinner, perhaps even going from table to table taking drink orders and other requests. Sometimes, I'll even help serve the dinners, all the while getting to know my audience — and gathering more "wood."

I've found that these are fantastic ways to connect with the audience and captivate them. I'll compliment them with specifics. I'll come to points in my speech where I'll stop and say:

— "Barbara Smith told me something earlier that I'd like to share with you."
Then, I'll ask Barbara to stand up and be recognized, as I share her comments, to the applause of her peers. I love when they applaud each other.

— "I had the privilege to meet Bill Johnson earlier tonight. Bill, please stand up for a moment, won't you? Bill won an award for outstanding customer service..." and thank him for his achievement. I will tell them what a difference they've made to me that night, and what a difference they've made in their departments and in their company. I've empowered them.

And I always try to stay after my speech, so that people have an opportunity to remain connected and be appreciated. People can come up to me and ask questions, give me their ideas, or discuss something I've said. I use their comments and evaluations for future speeches. The dynamics of one speech can inspire meaningful changes in the next one.

People are sharing.

People are connecting.

People are being inspired.

People are being recognized

People are feeling appreciated and loved.

People are realizing that their lives are making a difference!

When all this comes together, the title of this book breathes life.

"I'm on fire,

and when I speak

people come to watch me burn!"

...because I'm *burning for them!*

I mentioned near the beginning of this chapter that one of the most difficult times in my life was being with my dying mother as she suffered from cancer her last six months. I was with her throughout the last night of her life, and beside her for her last breath on the morning she died. I'll always cherish my last moments with Mom.

After the funeral, as we were sorting through her possessions, we found her diary. This amazing and profoundly moving memoir contains Mom's thoughts during her last days. I want to share one entry, an entry that made me proud.

It gave me peace...

and comfort...

Thank you, God, for showing me today that I can enjoy and accept the things people say I have done for them—or ways I have touched their lives—that this is your love poured on me to show me that my life did make a difference on this earth. What more could anyone want?

Mom was asking herself that third burning question. It's not something she ever discussed, but she surely was asking herself whether *she'd* made a difference.

And her answer?

"Yes!"

Conclusion

Build Your Own Fire!

Everyone is born a genius. Society degeniuses them.

—Buckminster Fuller

*T*his quote is sadly *too* true for far *too* many. We are habitual rule-followers. Both formal education and socialization work together to "drive us along with the herd." But it needn't be that way. We can regain our genius. But we can't achieve it by always following in another's footsteps.

"The man who follows the crowd," Alan Ashley-Pitts tells us, **"will usually get no further than the crowd."**

This entire book has led me to request this of you:

Be unique.

Develop your *own* style.

Break some rules, even ones that *I've* recommended.

I insist!

Recapture your genius. And when we couple courage and risk-taking, that genius will manifest itself in our presentations.

> **Children enter school as question marks and come out as periods.**
>
> —**Neil Postman**

Rid yourself of "periods" and any other conforming punctuation.

Dare to be different.

> **Dare to be very different.**

> **Dare to be yourself.**

From Dave Schwenson's book, *How to Be a Comedian:*

> **You should never sit down. This is a "stand up" comedy.**
> (*Yeah? Try telling that to Bill Cosby.*)
>
> **Don't do pratfalls or slapstick. It makes a comic look silly.**
> (*Are you listening, Jim Carrey and Michael Richards?*)
>
> **Center yourself at the middle of the stage and don't pace around. You'll keep the audience's attention better.**
> (*Do you think Robin Williams and Steven Wright would agree?*)

Be different!

> **Be yourself!**

Build your own fires!

Like the earth of a hundred years ago, our mind still has its darkest Africa, its unmapped Borneos and Amazonian basins.

—Aldous Huxley

There is perhaps no application of this quote more fitting than in the realm of speaking. How much has speaking *really* changed and improved in the last one hundred years?

Pause for a moment to consider the past 100 years:

How much has technology changed?

How much has health care changed?

How much has transportation changed?

How much has athletics changed?

How about speaking?

Has speaking changed *at all* in the past century?

We seem to be *still* hiding in the comfort of rules and traditions.

But we have unmapped territories to explore.

New communication horizons await us.

So, with this in mind,

!!*BreaK some rules*

Learn from others!

Take some risks!

Disclose!

Believe!

Honor!

Love!

BURN!

**...The greatest picture is not yet painted,
the greatest play isn't written,
the greatest poem is unsung.**

—Lincoln Steffens

The greatest speech has not yet been crafted.

The greatest speech has not yet been delivered.

Perhaps it's your destiny to do just that!

I only hope I am there to...

......watch you burn!

Thank you for allowing me the opportunity to share with you —

James